Generative AI for Finance

Building Agents for Research and Trading

Victor Trex

Published by NobleTrex Press

For permissions and other inquiries, write to:
P.O. Box 3132, Framingham, MA 01701, USA

Contents

1 Foundations for Quant Finance and AI **5**

1.1 Quantitative Programming Foundations 5
1.2 Mathematical Fundamentals for AI in Finance 18
1.3 Financial Markets and Time Series Basics 30

2 Data Engineering and Machine Learning Core **41**

2.1 Data Pipelines and Governance for Market Data 41
2.2 Compute Infrastructure and Performance Engineering 52
2.3 Supervised & Unsupervised Learning Foundations . . . 63
2.4 Reinforcement Learning Essentials 73

3 Generative Models, Retrieval, and Knowledge Systems **85**

3.1 Transformer Architecture and Domain Adaptation . . . 85
3.2 Embeddings and Vector Indexing 97
3.3 Prompt Engineering and Long-Context Techniques . . 108
3.4 Retrieval-Augmented Generation and Knowledge Graphs 119

4 Agentic Systems and Orchestration **133**

4.1 Agent Design Patterns and Control Loops 133
4.2 Tool Integration and Function Calling 146

4.3 Multi-agent Coordination and Planning 157
4.4 Memory, Budgeting, and Operational Control 170

5 Evaluation, MLOps, and Governance **181**
5.1 LLM and Agent Evaluation 181
5.2 Backtesting and Market Simulation 193
5.3 MLOps, Deployment, and Monitoring 204
5.4 Risk Management, Compliance, and Security 217

6 Applications: Research Agents **229**
6.1 Information Extraction from Financial Documents . . . 229
6.2 Event and Sentiment-Driven Signal Generation 243
6.3 Scenario Generation and Report Automation 255

7 Applications: Trading Agents **267**
7.1 Strategy Design and Portfolio Construction 267
7.2 Execution Agents and Market Microstructure 278
7.3 Reinforcement Learning and Adaptive Trading 289

Introduction

Generative models have moved from novelty to necessity in modern quantitative finance. What began as advances in sequence modeling and representation learning now enables systems that read filings, reason over market context, compose analytical workflows, and act through tools with measurable discipline. This book-Generative AI for Finance: Building Agents for Research and Trading-takes that shift seriously. Rather than treating large language models as isolated predictors, we present a blueprint for constructing agentic systems that are grounded in data, aligned with governance, and engineered for performance under real market constraints.

Our central thesis is simple: useful financial AI must be more than clever text generation. It must integrate three pillars-sound quantitative foundations, robust data and compute infrastructure, and agent architectures that can plan, retrieve, decide, and execute. The result is a practitioner's path from principles to production, with attention to the details that determine whether a prototype scales: provenance tracking, cost and latency budgets, memory strategies, error handling, and evaluation protocols that tie offline metrics to business outcomes.

This book is written for quantitative researchers, data scientists, software and infrastructure engineers, and risk and compliance professionals who need common language and shared tooling. Readers comfortable with Python and basic probability will benefit immediately; those newer to market structure or machine learning can leverage the early chapters to establish the required baseline. Throughout, we emphasize reproducibility and clarity over hype: modular code organization, deterministic pipelines, unit and integration testing, and documentation that survives model and data drift.

The structure of the book reflects the lifecycle of building and operating financial agents. We begin with the foundations you will draw on repeatedly: programming discipline for reproducible research, the mathematical toolkit behind uncertainty estimation and optimization, and a concise orientation to asset classes, microstructure, and time-series dynamics. We then build the data engineering and learning core: ingestion and governance for market data, performant cloud and on-prem compute choices, and the supervised, unsupervised, and reinforcement learning paradigms that later support generative modeling and adaptive control.

With those building blocks in place, we turn to the generative stack itself: the transformer architecture and domain adaptation techniques; embeddings and vector indexes for low-latency retrieval; prompting and long-context strategies that balance cost with fidelity; and retrieval-augmented generation with knowledge graphs to anchor outputs in verifiable facts. From there, we make the leap from models to systems. You will design single- and multi-agent control loops; integrate tools and deterministic function calls to expose analytics, data queries, and execution venues; and implement memory, budgeting, and operational guardrails so that agents remain efficient, auditable, and aligned with policy.

Engineering does not end at first success. We devote a full arc to evaluation, MLOps, and governance: task suites that diagnose reasoning and grounding; backtests and event-driven simulators that approximate real market frictions; CI/CD pipelines, registries, and telemetry that support safe iteration; and risk management and security practices that confront model risk, prompt injection, privacy, and access control. The goal is not simply to "ship an agent," but to operate one responsibly over time.

The final two parts of the book bring the framework to life. On the research side, you will build document agents that parse filings, earnings calls, and news into structured, cited facts; transform events and sentiment into leakage-controlled signals; and automate scenario generation and report drafting with traceable provenance. On the trading side, you will assemble strategies from multiple alphas under capacity and risk constraints; construct execution agents attuned to liquidity and impact; and explore reinforcement learning and online adaptation to remain robust as regimes shift.

Two commitments run through every chapter. First, grounding: agents should show their work with sources, data lineage, and interpretable intermediate states. Second, constraints: budget, latency, compliance, and reliability are first-class design objectives, not afterthoughts. Where trade-offs are unavoidable, we make them explicit and provide patterns to measure, monitor, and revisit decisions as conditions change.

A final note on scope and responsibility. The techniques presented here are for education and engineering practice; they do not constitute investment advice. Financial data is noisy, adversarial, and non-stationary. Any system you deploy must be validated against your organization's policies, legal obligations, and risk appetite. Treat evaluation and governance as enabling capabilities, not brakes.

By the end of this book, you will be able to architect and implement research and trading agents that are data-grounded, tool-using, evaluable, and secure. More importantly, you will have a method: a way to connect quantitative insight, generative intelligence, and operational rigor into systems that earn trust-one tested assumption, one documented decision, and one measured improvement at a time.

Chapter 1

Foundations for Quant Finance and AI

Before we let generative models write research code or trade on our behalf, we need a common language: a way to think in vectors and probabilities, a feel for how markets actually behave, and the engineering discipline to turn ideas into reliable systems. This chapter gives you that foundation. We move from clean, testable Python for quantitative work, through the core math that powers modern AI, into the structure and dynamics of real financial markets and time series-so that every agent you build later in the book rests on solid ground instead of guesswork and folklore.

1.1 Quantitative Programming Foundations

The previous chapter equipped you with the financial and mathematical language needed to read models, think about uncertainty, and interpret time series. In this section, we shift from *what* to *how*: how to turn those ideas into code that you can trust.

In quantitative finance and AI-driven trading, a large fraction of failures do not come from exotic math; they come from messy code, hidden assumptions, and experiments that cannot be reproduced. A professional-grade Python workflow is therefore not a luxury—it is your primary risk control for research.

Our goal in this section is to turn Python from a quick scripting tool into a robust platform for quantitative research and agent development. We will focus on three themes:

- **Readability**: code that you and your colleagues can understand months later.
- **Reproducibility**: experiments that can be rerun and verified, with clear inputs and outputs.
- **Reliability**: numerical results that are tested, logged, and monitored so that you trust them enough to deploy.

We will build up these ideas gradually: first by choosing a sensible technical stack and project layout, then by introducing disciplined use of notebooks, configuration and logging, testing strategies for numerical and stochastic code, and finally simple performance practices and an MLOps mindset that anticipates moving from research to production.

From Ad-Hoc Scripts to Research Projects

Most people begin with a single notebook or script. For quick exploration this is fine, but three problems appear quickly in quant finance and AI:

- **Everything is tangled.** Data loading, feature engineering, modeling, and plotting all live in one long file.
- **Nothing can be repeated.** Changing one cell or line modifies global state in unpredictable ways; running the notebook from top to bottom twice may not yield the same results.
- **No clear boundaries.** You cannot easily reuse a data-cleaning function across projects, or test a risk metric independently from your trading logic.

To move beyond this, you need to think like a small software team, even if you are working alone. The key shift is to treat your research codebase as a *project* with a clear structure, not as a pile of one-off experiments.

A simple mental model is to separate:

- **Interface**: notebooks, command line interfaces, or APIs that you or other agents use to run experiments.
- **Library**: reusable Python modules for data, features, models, and agent logic.
- **Infrastructure**: environment setup, dependencies, configuration, logging, and tests.

This basic separation is what will allow your generative AI agents later in the book to call into a stable library rather than having to reason about arbitrary notebooks.

A Practical Python Stack for Quant and AI

Before structuring a project, you need a consistent Python environment. The specifics will evolve, but the principles are stable.

Python and environment management

For quantitative finance and AI you will typically rely on:

- **Core language**: recent versions of Python 3 (for example 3.11+).
- **Numerical stack**: NumPy, pandas, SciPy.
- **Plotting**: matplotlib, possibly seaborn or plotly for richer visuals.
- **Machine learning**: scikit-learn for classical models; PyTorch or TensorFlow for deep learning; specialized libraries for time series as needed.

The critical step is to isolate each project's dependencies. Using the system-wide Python installation invites version conflicts and non-reproducible results. Instead, use virtual environments (such as venv, conda, or poetry environments). Conceptually, a virtual environment is a private Python world just for your project: it has its own interpreter and installed packages.

Freezing dependencies

Reproducibility requires that other people—and your future self—can recreate the same environment. The usual approach is to record dependencies in a file such as requirements.txt or a pyproject.toml. The key idea is simple: your project specifies not "any version of pandas" but precisely which major versions were used when you ran the experiments.

In a trading context, a subtle bug introduced by an unpinned dependency can propagate into P&L. By freezing versions, you reduce one more source of uncertainty in your workflow.

Organizing a Quant Research Repository

Once your environment is stable, the next step is to choose a project layout that reflects how you think about your work. A minimal but effective structure for a quant and AI project is:

- data/: raw and processed data files, possibly with subfolders like raw/, interim/, features/.
- notebooks/: exploratory analyses, visualizations, and experiment front-ends.
- src/yourproject/: the main Python package with modules such as data_loading, features, models, agents, evaluation.
- configs/: configuration files describing experiments or environments.
- tests/: unit and property-based tests.

- scripts/: small command-line entry points for running backtests or training jobs.

The important concept is separation of concerns:

- Data ingestion and cleaning live in a dedicated place and can be tested independently.
- Feature engineering is expressed as a library of transformations rather than being buried in notebook cells.
- Model training, evaluation, and agent logic are written as functions or classes in src/, not only as one-off scripts.

This layout mirrors the lifecycle of any trading or research pipeline: from data to features, to models, to decisions and evaluation. It is also what will allow later chapters on agentic systems and MLOps to plug into your work with minimal changes.

Using Notebooks as Front Ends, Not as the System

Jupyter notebooks are powerful tools for visual exploration, diagnostics, and communication. They let you quickly inspect a return series, visualize autocorrelation, or prototype a new loss function. However, if you place all your logic in notebooks, you inherit several dangers:

- Execution order can be arbitrary, leading to hidden state and non-reproducible results.
- It is hard to test individual pieces of logic automatically.
- Version control becomes noisy because notebooks mix code, output, and formatting.

A professional workflow treats notebooks as *clients* of a well-structured Python library. The pattern is:

- Implement core functionality (for example, a function that computes volatility features or runs a backtest) in src/yourproject/.

- Import those functions into notebooks and use them to explore results, visualize diagnostics, or run small experiments.
- Whenever a notebook cell grows into something that might be reused, move it into the library and keep the notebook thin.

This pattern brings several benefits:

- You can run the same logic from the command line, from an automated test, or from an AI agent, without copying code.
- Your notebooks read more like documented scenarios: "load configuration, run experiment, plot results".
- You reduce the chance that a silent side effect in one cell contaminates another experiment.

In later chapters, when we build agentic systems that orchestrate research and trading tasks, those agents will rely on being able to call your library functions directly, without needing to run notebooks.

Configuration Management for Reproducible Experiments

Quantitative research often involves running many variations of an experiment: different universes of assets, different lookback windows, different hyperparameters for a model, or different assumptions about transaction costs.

If each of these setups is hardcoded in Python or scattered across notebooks, you will struggle to:

- Explain exactly what was run.
- Reproduce a promising result with slightly changed inputs.
- Compare experiments in a systematic way.

Configuration management solves this by moving experiment details into explicit configuration files. Practically, this might mean using simple formats like YAML or JSON to describe:

- Data sources and time ranges (for example, "daily prices from 2010–2020 for S&P 500 constituents").
- Feature settings (lag windows, volatility horizons, normalization choices).
- Model hyperparameters (learning rates, number of layers, regularization strengths).
- Backtest parameters (transaction costs, slippage assumptions, capital constraints).

Your experiment runner (a notebook or command-line script) then reads a configuration file and executes the entire pipeline deterministically. The benefit is conceptual: rather than thinking "I clicked these cells in this order", you think "I ran configuration X on code version Y". That is the language of reproducible science and auditable trading research.

Logging and Experiment Tracking

In live markets, you cannot go back in time. In your code, you should act similarly: once an experiment is run, its key inputs and outputs should be recorded so you can reconstruct what happened.

At a minimum, logging should capture:

- Which configuration was used.
- Which code version or commit hash was executed.
- Key metrics (for example, Sharpe ratio, maximum drawdown, hit rate, training loss curves).
- Any warnings or errors that occurred during the run.

In Python, logging libraries provide a structured way to record messages with timestamps and severity levels. For richer experiment tracking, later chapters will introduce tools that store metrics and artifacts centrally. For now, the conceptual shift matters: you no longer treat a research run as a one-off; you treat it as a documented event with a trail.

This is especially important for AI-driven agents that may run many experiments automatically. Without logs and clear experiment identifiers, you cannot safely trust or debug their outputs.

Testing Numerical and Stochastic Code

In quant finance, logic bugs often look like plausible but wrong numbers. A backtest that double-counts cash flows or misaligns returns by one day may still produce smooth equity curves. Testing is therefore a core ingredient of reliability.

Unit tests for numerical code

Unit tests check small pieces of code in isolation. For example, you might test that:

- A function converting prices to log-returns handles missing values and corporate actions as expected.
- A risk metric such as volatility or Value-at-Risk behaves correctly on simple, synthetic data.
- A position update function correctly applies trades, transaction costs, and constraints.

The mindset to adopt is this: if a function transforms data in a nontrivial way, you should be able to describe a few small input cases where you know the correct answer by hand. Encoding those cases as tests creates a safety net: refactors or performance optimizations can be made with confidence that you are not silently changing financial meaning.

Property-based and stochastic testing

AI models and trading simulations often involve randomness: random initialization of weights, bootstrapped samples, Monte Carlo paths for prices, or stochastic policies for exploration. Testing these components requires a slightly different idea: instead of checking a single expected output, you check properties that should hold across many random draws.

Examples of useful properties include:

- Simulated price paths should not produce negative prices if you are modeling assets that cannot go below zero.
- The distribution of simulated returns should have means and variances within a reasonable range.
- Re-running a stochastic process with the same random seed should yield identical results.

These tests do not guarantee correctness in a formal sense, but they rule out broad classes of errors. For generative AI models, you can similarly test that generated sequences respect constraints (for example, orders do not exceed available liquidity, or positions stay within bounds). As your agents become more complex, these property-based tests will be among your most valuable tools.

Performance-Aware Coding and Vectorization

In the previous chapter, you saw how financial time series can be long, noisy, and high-dimensional. AI models that operate on such data, especially in multi-asset settings, can be computationally heavy. However, not every performance issue requires a complex solution.

Start with profiling, not guessing

Before optimizing, you should know where time is actually spent. Profiling tools answer questions like: which function takes most of the runtime? Is the bottleneck in Python loops, data access, model training, or logging?

The principle is simple: measure first, optimize second. Many perceived performance issues turn out to be the wrong target; for instance, elaborate optimizations in model code might be irrelevant if the real bottleneck is reading data from disk or repeatedly calculating the same features.

Vectorization and avoiding unnecessary loops

For many operations on time series and matrices, vectorized code using NumPy, pandas, or similar libraries is both faster and easier to reason about than manual loops. Thinking in vectorized terms means:

- Operating on whole arrays or columns at once instead of row by row.
- Using built-in rolling, expanding, and grouping operations rather than writing nested loops.
- Leveraging linear algebra formulations where possible, which tie back to the linear algebra concepts from the previous chapter.

For example, computing rolling volatility for many assets at once is typically more efficient and less error-prone when expressed as an operation on a matrix of returns rather than writing loops over assets and time.

When to use just-in-time compilation or parallelization

There are cases—especially with custom simulations, order book modeling, or complex agent logic—where vectorization alone is not enough. Just-in-time (JIT) compilation tools or parallel processing libraries can speed up hot loops significantly.

The guideline is conservative: reach for these tools only after you have:

- Verified correctness with thorough tests.
- Identified a real bottleneck through profiling.
- Confirmed that vectorization and simple algorithmic improvements are not sufficient.

This ordering preserves reliability: correctness first, performance second. In a trading environment, a fast wrong answer is far worse than a slow correct one.

A Lightweight MLOps Mindset for Quant Research

MLOps, at its core, is about turning machine learning from fragile experiments into reliable systems. In this book, we focus on a lightweight flavor appropriate for quant research desks and small teams. The themes you have already seen—environment management, configuration, logging, and testing—are all part of that story.

Three additional ideas round out the picture:

Version-controlling code, data, and models

You are likely already familiar with version control for code. In quantitative finance and AI, it is equally important to keep track of which data and which model artifacts correspond to which code versions.

This does not mean you must put gigabytes of data in a source repository. Instead, you might:

- Store metadata about data snapshots (for example, dates, vendors, filters) alongside code.
- Name model files and results in ways that reference both experiment identifiers and code versions.
- Keep a simple catalog that maps "model X" to the configurations and inputs that created it.

This discipline ensures that when a particular model or backtest result attracts attention (good or bad), you can trace it back precisely.

Designing for deployment from the start

Even if you are currently in pure research mode, it helps to write code with an eye toward eventual deployment. Practically, this means:

- Avoiding tight coupling between data access and modeling logic. Agents in production may consume data from streaming sources rather than local files.

- Encapsulating model inference and decision logic in clear interfaces that can be plugged into different environments (backtests, paper trading, live execution).

- Keeping side effects (like writing to disk or sending orders) separate from pure computation, to allow for easy testing and simulation.

By doing so, you minimize painful rewrites later, when you want to take a successful generative AI agent from a prototype notebook into a live or semi-live environment.

Documenting experiments and assumptions

Finally, a professional-grade workflow includes clear documentation of what each experiment or agent is attempting to do and under what assumptions. This does not require long essays; concise notes about:

- The research question (for example, "Can a sequence model using limit order book snapshots predict short-term direction better than a simple volatility filter?").

- The data regime (assets, time periods, market conditions).

- The modeling approach and key hyperparameters.

- Known limitations or caveats.

This habit prevents misinterpretation and overgeneralization of results. It also helps future collaborators—including future AI agents that may read and reason about your reports—to understand the boundaries within which a model or strategy was validated.

Bringing It All Together

Quantitative programming foundations are not about adopting a specific framework or tool; they are about adopting a way of working. The core ideas in this section can be summarized as follows:

- Treat your quant and AI projects as structured software systems, not as collections of ad-hoc scripts.
- Use virtual environments and pinned dependencies to ensure that your experiments are reproducible.
- Organize your repository so that data pipelines, feature engineering, models, and agents live in clear, testable modules.
- Use notebooks as user interfaces, not as the primary home for logic.
- Externalize experiment details into configuration files and record runs through logging and simple experiment tracking.
- Protect yourself against subtle numerical errors with unit and property-based tests, especially for stochastic components.
- Address performance with measurement, vectorization, and carefully considered optimization, always prioritizing correctness.
- Adopt a lightweight MLOps mindset that anticipates versioning, deployment, and documentation from the beginning.

These practices form the bridge between the mathematical and financial foundations you have already learned and the generative AI and agentic systems you will build next. With this groundwork in place, your models and agents will not only be sophisticated, but also maintainable, auditable, and ready for real-world trading and research environments.

1.2 Mathematical Fundamentals for AI in Finance

In the previous section, we focused on building a professional programming workflow: how to organize code, manage experiments, and keep your research reproducible. In this section, we turn to the mathematical language that your code will speak.

Our goal is not to turn you into a pure mathematician. Instead, we want to give you an intuitive toolkit: enough probability, statistics, linear algebra, calculus, and optimization to understand how modern models behave, where their strengths and weaknesses come from, and how to reason about risk and uncertainty in a disciplined way.

Think of this section as a map of the terrain rather than a full encyclopedia. You will see each mathematical area connected directly to concrete finance and AI tasks: risk estimation, portfolio representation, gradient-based training, and the design and evaluation of generative models and agents.

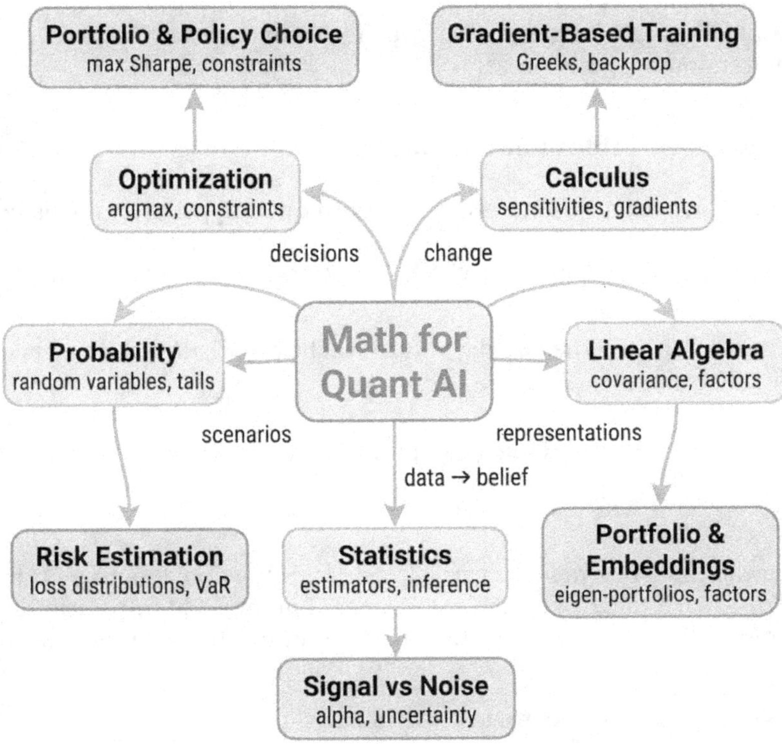

We will walk this map clockwise: starting with probability and statistics, then moving through linear algebra, calculus, and optimization. Along the way, we will keep returning to the same guiding questions:

- How uncertain is this quantity (P&L, risk, model output)?
- How should I represent my data or portfolio?
- How does a small change in something (a parameter, an input, a price) change an output?
- Given competing choices, which one is best under my objective and constraints?

Probability: Describing Uncertainty

Probability is the language we use to talk about uncertain future events and random variation in data.

Random variables and scenarios

A *random variable* is simply a numerical quantity whose value is uncertain. Tomorrow's return on a stock, the time until the next market order arrives, and the future P&L of a strategy over one week are all random variables.

Instead of saying "the one-day return will be 0.4%", probability lets us say things like:

- There is a 60% chance the return will lie between -1% and $+1\%$.
- There is a 5% chance the loss will exceed 2%.

You can think of a random variable as a machine that assigns a probability to each range of possible outcomes. Running a Monte Carlo simulation is like drawing many hypothetical futures from this machine.

Distributions, expectations, and tails

The *distribution* of a random variable tells you how likely various outcomes are. For financial returns, we often care about:

- **Center**: commonly described by the mean or median; this is your expected return.
- **Spread**: often measured by variance or standard deviation; this relates to volatility.
- **Tails**: how fat or thin the extremes are; this matters for crash risk and large drawdowns.

The *expected value* (or expectation) is a probability-weighted average of all possible outcomes. In risk terms, it is the "average" P&L over many hypothetical worlds. But risk management is about more than averages; the tails, where rare but large losses live, are often where portfolios break.

This is why quant finance pays attention to tail-sensitive measures like Value-at-Risk (VaR) or expected shortfall, which are directly related to quantiles of the loss distribution.

Conditional probability and dependence

Markets are not memoryless. The probability of a large move often depends on current volatility, macro conditions, or news. *Conditional probability* captures this: it asks, "Given that some event has occurred, what is the probability of another event?"

For example:

- The probability of a credit default given that spreads have widened significantly.
- The probability of a large intraday move given that realized volatility over the last week is high.

Conditional reasoning is central in AI models as well: a generative price model might specify the probability of tomorrow's returns given today's state, and an LLM-based research assistant may reason about the likelihood of scenarios given observed news.

Statistics: Learning From Data

Probability tells you what could happen in theory. Statistics tells you what you can infer from the data you actually observe.

Estimators and sampling variation

Suppose you observe 1,000 daily returns and compute their average. That average is an *estimate* of the unknown true mean return. If you had drawn a different 1,000-day window, you would have obtained a slightly different average. This is sampling variation.

An *estimator* is a rule for turning data into a number (for example, "take the average" or "take the median"). Statistics asks:

- Is the estimator *biased* (systematically too high or too low)?
- How variable is it if I repeated the sampling?
- How confident can I be that the true quantity lies in a certain range?

In finance, this matters whenever you report a Sharpe ratio, a correlation, or a model's accuracy. These are not exact truths; they are estimates that come with uncertainty.

Confidence intervals and "is this alpha real?"

A *confidence interval* gives a range of plausible values for an unknown parameter, like the mean excess return of a strategy. Instead of saying "the Sharpe ratio is 1.2", you might say "with 95% confidence, the Sharpe ratio lies between 0.7 and 1.7".

For AI-driven trading, this helps answer critical questions:

- Is this apparent alpha likely to be real, or could it easily have arisen by chance?
- How wide is the uncertainty around my forecast of next month's volatility?

When you train many models or explore many signals, some will look good purely by accident. Statistical thinking helps you avoid overreacting to lucky noise.

Hypothesis testing and model comparison

A *hypothesis test* is a structured way to ask, "Does the data provide enough evidence to reject a simple explanation?" Examples:

- Null hypothesis: "This signal has zero predictive power." Does your backtest performance significantly exceed what we would expect under pure noise?
- Null hypothesis: "Model A and Model B have equal accuracy." Does one model perform meaningfully better than the other across many time periods or assets?

In practice, you will not perform formal tests for every idea. But the underlying habit—asking whether an observed pattern is robust vs. a statistical fluke—is essential for responsible use of generative and predictive models.

Linear Algebra: Representing Portfolios and Models

If probability and statistics are how we reason about uncertainty, linear algebra is how we represent and manipulate collections of numbers: portfolios, factor exposures, embedding vectors, and network weights.

Vectors and matrices as containers

A *vector* is an ordered list of numbers. You can think of:

- A portfolio of n assets as an n-dimensional vector of weights.
- A snapshot of the limit order book as a high-dimensional vector of volumes at each price level.
- An embedding of a research document as a vector in a semantic space.

A *matrix* is a rectangular array of numbers. In quant finance, you often see:

- Price or return matrices: each row is a time point, each column an asset.
- Covariance matrices, summarizing how returns co-move.

- Factor loading matrices that map from factors to asset returns.

Modern AI models are also largely matrix machines: they take vectors in, apply matrix operations, and produce new vectors.

Covariance, correlation, and factor structure

The covariance matrix of returns is central in both risk management and portfolio construction. Each entry tells you how two assets move together. Intuitively:

- Large positive covariance: assets often move in the same direction.
- Large negative covariance: they tend to offset each other.
- Near-zero covariance: movements are mostly unrelated.

This structure lets you ask: how much risk comes from broad market movements vs. idiosyncratic noise? Factor models approximate the return vector as a combination of a few common factors plus noise. Mathematically, this is a matrix equation; intuitively, it says "these five or ten driving forces explain most of what happens."

Eigenvalues, eigenvectors, and "eigen-portfolios"

Eigenvalues and eigenvectors arise when you ask: in which directions does a transformation stretch or compress space the most? Applied to covariance matrices, eigenvectors correspond to special portfolios (sometimes called eigen-portfolios or principal components) whose returns are uncorrelated with each other, and eigenvalues measure how much variance each explains.

This is not just an abstract idea. In practice:

- PCA (principal component analysis) on bond returns often reveals level, slope, and curvature factors.
- Dimensionality reduction via eigen-decomposition helps denoise estimates and simplify models.

In deep learning, similar linear algebra concepts appear in the analysis of weight matrices and attention mechanisms. While you may not compute eigenvalues by hand, understanding that they describe dominant directions of variation helps in interpreting models and risks.

Calculus: Sensitivities and Gradients

Calculus, in this context, is about understanding how a small change in an input or parameter changes an output.

Derivatives as sensitivities

A *derivative* measures sensitivity. For example:

- How does the value of an option change if the underlying price moves up slightly? This is Delta.
- How does your portfolio P&L change if interest rates shift by a few basis points?
- How does a model's loss change if you adjust a weight slightly?

Thinking in sensitivities is essential both for risk management (the Greeks in derivatives) and for AI training (gradients of loss functions).

Partial derivatives and many variables

Most quantities in finance and AI depend on many inputs at once: prices, volatilities, correlations, and model parameters. A *partial derivative* isolates the effect of changing one variable while holding others fixed.

The collection of all partial derivatives of a function with respect to its inputs is called the *gradient*. You can picture the gradient as an arrow in input space, pointing in the direction where the function increases most rapidly.

Backpropagation and gradient flow

Training neural networks relies on calculating gradients of the loss with respect to millions of parameters. Doing this by hand is impossible. Instead, automatic differentiation uses the chain rule—a basic calculus idea that describes how the derivative of a composed function can be built from derivatives of its parts—to propagate gradients backward through the network.

You do not need to memorize the details of backpropagation algorithms, but it is important to understand:

- Gradient-based training works by nudging parameters a tiny bit in the direction that reduces loss.
- Vanishing or exploding gradients (where sensitivities shrink or blow up as you go deeper) can cause training difficulties; architectural choices are often aimed at controlling this.

Later, when you tune or debug generative models or reinforcement learning agents, you will frequently reason in terms of gradients: is the model receiving clear, stable signals about how to improve?

Optimization: Turning Models and Views into Decisions

Once you can represent your data (linear algebra) and understand how outputs respond to changes (calculus), you are ready for optimization: the systematic search for the best choice under an objective and constraints.

Objectives, constraints, and trade-offs

An optimization problem has three main ingredients:

- **Decision variables**: what you control (portfolio weights, model parameters, policy actions).

- **Objective**: what you want to optimize (expected return, risk-adjusted return, prediction error, utility).

- **Constraints**: what limits your choices (capital, risk limits, liquidity, regulations).

In traditional portfolio optimization, you might choose weights to maximize expected return for a given level of risk, or minimize risk subject to a target return. In model training, you choose parameters to minimize a loss function that penalizes prediction errors and perhaps model complexity.

Convex vs. nonconvex landscapes

The *shape* of the objective function matters. Roughly:

- **Convex** problems (with a single bowl-shaped minimum) are well-behaved: any local optimum is global, and efficient algorithms exist.

- **Nonconvex** problems (with many hills and valleys) can have many local optima; gradient-based methods may find different solutions depending on initialization.

Classical mean-variance portfolio optimization is convex under certain assumptions, which is why it is relatively tractable. Deep neural network training, in contrast, is highly nonconvex, yet gradient-based methods work surprisingly well in practice.

As an AI practitioner in finance, you rarely derive these properties from scratch, but you should be aware that:

- Some optimization problems offer strong guarantees; others do not.

- Regularization and good initialization often help navigate complicated landscapes.

Gradient descent and its variants

The workhorse of modern model training is gradient descent: iteratively move the parameters in the direction opposite the gradient of the loss. Intuitively:

- Compute how the loss changes with respect to each parameter (the gradient).
- Take a small step in the direction that reduces the loss.
- Repeat many times until changes are small or performance levels off.

Variants like stochastic gradient descent (SGD) and adaptive methods (Adam, RMSprop, and others) use mini-batches of data and adjust step sizes automatically. For you, the key practical lever is learning rate and related hyperparameters: too large, and you overshoot and diverge; too small, and training is painfully slow or stuck.

Regularization and overfitting control

Optimization in AI is almost always done under data constraints: you have a finite, noisy sample from a complex, changing market. A highly flexible model can fit the noise—appearing impressive in-sample but failing out-of-sample.

Regularization combats this by adding penalties or constraints that prefer simpler or more stable solutions. Examples include:

- Adding a penalty on large parameter values (L2 regularization).
- Encouraging sparsity in weights (L1 regularization).
- Constraining portfolio weights (for example, limiting leverage or turnover).

From a Bayesian viewpoint, regularization encodes prior beliefs about what models or portfolios are reasonable. From an engineering viewpoint, it is one of your main tools for making AI agents robust rather than fragile.

Connecting Back to Models and Agents

We have briefly toured the five main mathematical pillars:

- **Probability** describes uncertain scenarios and tail risks.
- **Statistics** tells you how much you can infer from limited data.
- **Linear algebra** provides the language for representing portfolios, covariances, and model internals.
- **Calculus** gives you sensitivities and gradients, the basis for risk measures and learning.
- **Optimization** turns beliefs and models into concrete decisions within constraints.

Later chapters will build generative models, retrieval-augmented systems, and agentic workflows on top of this foundation. As you encounter new techniques, you will repeatedly see the same patterns:

- A probabilistic description of data or rewards.
- Statistical estimation or inference from historical samples.
- Linear transformations of high-dimensional vectors.
- Gradients flowing through networks or decision rules.
- Optimization of an objective under real-world constraints and risks.

You do not need to master every theorem. But if you develop a comfortable, intuitive grasp of these ideas, you will be able to read model documentation critically, debug training issues, and collaborate effectively with both quants and machine learning engineers—and, importantly, design AI trading agents that are not only clever, but also well-grounded in the realities of uncertainty and risk.

1.3 Financial Markets and Time Series Basics

So far we have set up two pillars for building AI in finance. You now have a disciplined programming workflow and an intuitive mathematical toolkit. The next question is: *what kind of world will your models and agents live in?*

This section answers that by grounding us in real markets and the data they produce. We will:

- Sketch the main asset classes and what makes each structurally different.
- Look inside markets at the level of orders and trades (market microstructure).
- Introduce financial time series: prices, returns, volatility, and dependence over time.
- Highlight empirical features—like volatility clustering and regime shifts—that any serious model or AI agent must respect.
- Call out common data pitfalls that quietly break backtests and evaluations.

The aim is not encyclopedic coverage, but to give you a mental model of markets as dynamic systems that generate noisy, path-dependent time series. Your AI agents will be evaluated in this environment, not in an idealized textbook world.

A Quick Tour of Major Asset Classes

Financial markets trade many types of instruments. At a high level, you can think of four broad buckets. Understanding their differences helps you choose sensible data, labels, and modeling approaches.

Equities

Equities are ownership claims on firms. Their key features:

- **Payoffs**: uncertain and open-ended; you participate in future profits (and losses).
- **Information flow**: company news, macro indicators, flows from large investors.
- **Liquidity**: varies widely; large developed-market stocks are very liquid, small caps less so.

For AI agents, equity markets offer rich cross-sectional structure (many names, sectors, factors) and long histories, but also regime shifts linked to macro cycles and technological change.

Fixed income

Fixed income instruments (bonds, notes, bills) are debt claims: promises to pay coupons and principal.

- **Payoffs**: structured, with known schedules but uncertain default risk and interest rate risk.
- **Term structure**: instruments differ by maturity; yield curves encode expectations and risk premia.
- **Sensitivity**: strongly influenced by rates, credit spreads, and central bank policy.

Time series in fixed income often involve yields and spreads, which behave differently from equity prices: they are bounded in some directions, can be highly persistent, and interact through no-arbitrage relationships.

Foreign exchange (FX)

FX markets trade currency pairs (e.g., EUR/USD). Their characteristics:

- **Always relative**: a "price" is the value of one currency in terms of another.
- **Continuous trading**: major pairs trade nearly 24/5 with deep liquidity.

- **Macro-driven**: influenced by interest rate differentials, trade flows, geopolitical events.

FX returns tend to be heavy-tailed with episodes of extreme moves, which matters for any agent modeling risk or sizing trades.

Commodities and derivatives

Commodities (oil, metals, agricultural products) and derivatives (options, futures, swaps) are more specialized. Two features are especially important:

- **Term structures and curves**: futures prices across maturities form curves with shapes (contango, backwardation) that change over time.
- **Nonlinear payoffs**: options and many structured products have payoffs that are nonlinear functions of underlying prices, making Greeks and path dependence central.

For AI agents, derivatives add an extra layer: you model both underlying dynamics and the mapping from those dynamics to option prices and hedging costs.

Market Microstructure: How Orders Become Trades

From a distance, a market looks like a time series of prices and volumes. Up close, it is a continuous process of orders arriving, being matched, and sometimes canceled. For algorithmic agents, this microstructure is the environment.

Limit order books and quotes

Most modern electronic markets use a *limit order book*. Participants submit:

- **Limit orders**: orders to buy or sell at a specified price or better, which rest in the book until filled or canceled.

- **Market orders**: orders to buy or sell immediately at the best available price.

At any instant, the book contains:

- **Bids**: buy orders at various price levels.
- **Asks**: sell orders at various price levels.

The *best bid* is the highest buy price; the *best ask* is the lowest sell price. Their difference is the *bid-ask spread*. A trade occurs when a market order hits the resting liquidity at the top of the book, or when limit orders on opposite sides cross.

For AI systems that operate intraday or at high frequency, the state of the order book (depth, imbalance, spread) is a crucial part of the input.

Transaction costs, slippage, and latency

Realized P&L is not determined by mid-prices alone. Three frictions play a big role:

- **Transaction costs**: explicit fees (commissions, exchange fees, taxes).
- **Slippage**: the difference between your intended execution price and the actual price you receive, often due to limited liquidity or price impact.
- **Latency**: delays between observing market data, making a decision, and having your order reach the market.

An AI agent trained on clean price series but evaluated in a world with spreads, slippage, and latency may perform very differently than expected. Incorporating realistic execution models in your backtests and simulations is therefore essential.

From Prices to Returns

Most raw market data come as price and volume quotes. For modeling and risk measurement, we usually transform prices into *returns*.

Why returns, not prices?

Consider a stock that moves from 10 to 11, and later from 100 to 101. Both moves are a price change of 1, but the economic impact is very different. Returns capture proportional change:

- **Simple return**: roughly "percentage change" between two prices.
- **Log-return**: the logarithm of the price ratio, which composes nicely over time and is convenient in many models.

Working with returns usually makes the series closer to *stationary*: their properties (like average and variance) change more slowly over time than raw prices. This is important for many statistical methods that assume roughly stable distributions.

Levels vs. changes

Prices are typically *trending* and nonstationary: they wander, sometimes with clear drifts or regimes. Returns, especially over short horizons, often fluctuate around a mean closer to zero, with changing volatility.

This distinction echoes a theme from the math section: sometimes it is more informative to study differences or derivatives (returns, gradients) rather than absolute levels.

Basic Time Series Concepts

A financial time series is just an ordered sequence of observations through time: daily returns, intraday prices, trading volumes, or volatility estimates. But financial time series have distinctive features.

Autocorrelation: dependence over time

Autocorrelation measures how much a series is related to a lagged version of itself. Intuitively:

- If returns today are positively correlated with returns yesterday, there is *momentum* at that horizon.

- If they are negatively correlated, there is *mean reversion*.
- If correlation is near zero, returns at that lag behave almost like white noise.

In many liquid markets, returns themselves show weak autocorrelation at daily or longer horizons, but *squared* or *absolute* returns (proxies for volatility) show strong, persistent autocorrelation. This is one way to see *volatility clustering*.

Volatility clustering

Empirical financial data often show long stretches of relatively calm variation followed by periods of intense turbulence. This is volatility clustering: high-volatility days tend to be followed by high-volatility days, and low-volatility days by low-volatility days.

For AI agents, this matters because:

- Risk estimates that assume constant variance will be badly miscalibrated.
- Training distributions for models built in calm periods may not generalize to turbulent periods.
- Agents that adapt their risk-taking to perceived volatility (for example, scaling position sizes) can achieve more stable performance.

Stationarity and regime shifts

A process is *stationary* if its statistical properties (like mean and variance) do not change over time. Real markets are not fully stationary. They undergo:

- Structural breaks (for example, regulatory changes, new tick sizes, introduction of new instruments).
- Regime shifts (for example, from low- to high-inflation environments; from low-volatility bull markets to crisis regimes).

From a modeling perspective, it is sometimes useful to assume local stationarity: within a window of months or a few years, returns behave "as if" their distribution is stable. But agents should be designed with humility: the future may not look like the past, and abrupt changes can invalidate previously learned patterns.

Visualizing Core Time Series Features

Now that we have introduced prices vs. returns, autocorrelation, and volatility clustering, it is helpful to see them together in a single visual.

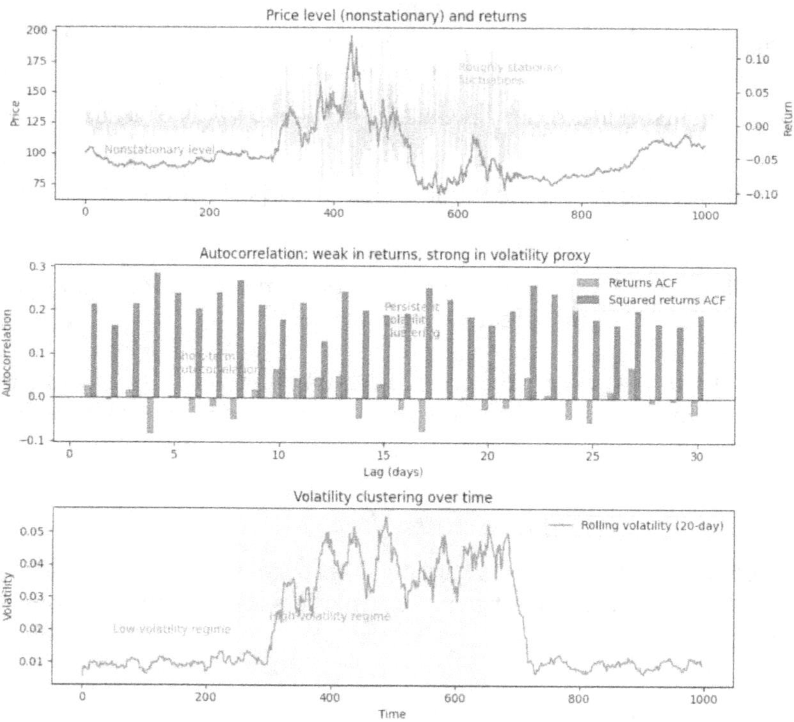

This synthetic example captures three key facts you should keep in the back of your mind when modeling:

- Price levels wander and trend; returns fluctuate around a relatively stable center.
- Raw returns often show little autocorrelation, but volatility proxies (squared or absolute returns) exhibit strong persistence.
- Volatility tends to cluster in time, with extended calm and stormy periods.

Real assets show these patterns in more complex and noisy ways, but the overall picture is robust across markets and time.

Irregular Sampling, Missing Data, and Market Calendars

Unlike simulated data, real financial time series are irregular and sometimes incomplete.

Trading calendars and gaps

Markets close on weekends and holidays, may halt trading during extreme events, and sometimes change their hours. This results in:

- Non-uniform gaps between timestamps (for example, Friday close to Monday close is a three-day interval).
- Variable numbers of trading days per month and per year.

When computing returns, volatilities, or features, it is important to account for this. Treating calendar days and trading days as interchangeable can distort horizons and risk estimates.

Missing and dirty data

You will frequently encounter:

- Missing prices (no trades for illiquid names, data vendor outages).
- Spurious spikes (bad ticks).

- Changes in identifiers due to corporate actions (splits, mergers, ticker changes).

Your earlier work on programming foundations becomes essential here: robust data-loading and cleaning functions, with tests and logging, are the first line of defense. AI agents are particularly sensitive to silent data problems; they can confidently learn from and act on corrupted inputs unless you protect against this.

Common Time Series Pitfalls in Research and AI Agents

Before closing, it is worth naming a few recurring pitfalls that appear in backtests and in AI-driven workflows.

Data leakage

Data leakage occurs when information from the future slips into the inputs for a prediction. Examples:

- Using end-of-day closing prices to predict same-day decisions as if they were known earlier.
- Constructing features (such as rolling means) using a symmetric window that includes future points.
- Training a model on data that has been filtered with knowledge of the full history (for example, using only assets that survive to the end).

Leakage often leads to surprisingly strong in-sample performance that vanishes in live trading. For AI agents that automatically construct features or call external tools, careful time-aware design and validation are crucial.

Survivorship and look-ahead biases

Survivorship bias arises when your universe only includes instruments that survived to the end of your sample (for example, current index constituents), ignoring delisted or bankrupt names. This can overstate historical performance and understate risk.

Look-ahead bias appears when you use information that was not actually available at the decision time (for example, revised earnings data or index membership defined later). Both biases are easy to introduce unintentionally and can seriously distort agent evaluation.

Structural breaks and nonstationarity

We noted earlier that markets change over time. A strategy or model trained in one regime may fail in another. Structural breaks—such as new trading rules, the introduction of decimal pricing, or major macro events—can:

- Change the distribution of returns and correlations.
- Alter liquidity and transaction costs.
- Render some previously powerful signals obsolete.

In an AI context, this means that task distributions are drifting. Techniques like rolling retraining, online learning, and explicit regime detection become important; but even before that, simply recognizing that "the data-generating process is not fixed" is a major step forward in designing realistic evaluations.

Putting It All Together

We have now sketched the world in which your generative models and agents will operate:

- Markets trade a variety of assets with distinct structures, constraints, and drivers.
- Under the hood, trades emerge from a continuous flow of orders in limit order books, subject to spreads, slippage, and latency.
- The raw output of this process is financial time series: prices, returns, volumes, and derived quantities like volatility.
- These series show persistent empirical features such as weak autocorrelation in returns, strong autocorrelation in volatility, volatility clustering, and regime shifts.

- Real data are messy: irregular sampling, missing values, corporate actions, and structural changes demand careful preprocessing and cautious interpretation.
- Common pitfalls like data leakage, survivorship bias, and ignoring structural breaks can invalidate even sophisticated AI-based strategies if left unchecked.

In the rest of this book, when we design generative models, retrieval-augmented systems, and agentic workflows, we will constantly return to this context. Every architectural choice, loss function, and evaluation metric should be interrogated with questions like:

- Does this respect the timing and information structure of real markets?
- Does it acknowledge the volatility and regime behavior we see in practice?
- Does it account for execution frictions and the true data-generating process?

By combining the mathematical tools from the previous section, the programming discipline from the start of the chapter, and the market realism captured here, you will be well-prepared to build AI agents that are not only clever in backtests, but also robust, interpretable, and aligned with how markets actually behave.

Chapter 2

Data Engineering and Machine Learning Core

Before you can trust a generative agent with research, risk, or trading decisions, you must first trust its data and its models. This chapter moves from the plumbing to the intelligence: we'll design market-grade data pipelines, tune the compute stack that powers training and inference, and build the core machine-learning foundations-supervised, unsupervised, and reinforcement learning-that make agentic systems in finance both powerful and safe.

2.1 Data Pipelines and Governance for Market Data

Generative agents for research and trading are only as good as the data they see. Before we can discuss clever models or sophisticated orchestration, we need to ensure that market data flows into your system in a way that is reliable, consistent, and auditable. In regulated financial environments, this is not a "nice to have" but a hard requirement: if you cannot explain exactly which data a model saw, how that data was transformed, and whether it was complete and correct at the time of a decision, your models are not production-ready.

In this section we build a conceptual and practical picture of an end-to-end market data pipeline. We start with the lifecycle of financial data, then walk from ingestion through transformation and quality control to storage and consumption. Alongside each step, we integrate governance, lineage, and auditability, so that the same pipeline can serve both classic machine learning (ML) workflows and generative or agentic systems introduced later in the book.

The Lifecycle of Financial Data

From the point of view of a trading or research organization, most financial data passes through a common lifecycle:

1. **Raw sources**: exchanges, trading venues, consolidated tapes, data vendors, internal trading systems, and alternative data providers.
2. **Ingestion**: collecting data from feeds or APIs, validating basic structure, and landing it into a controlled environment.
3. **Normalization and alignment**: enforcing common schemas, naming conventions, calendars, and time zones.
4. **Enrichment**: adding derived fields such as returns, spreads, or event labels; joining across datasets.
5. **Quality control**: detecting and resolving errors, gaps, and anomalies.
6. **Storage and access**: placing data into formats and systems that balance latency, cost, and regulatory obligations.
7. **Consumption**: powering backtests, factor research, real-time trading, risk dashboards, and now LLM- and agent-based workflows.

Governance overlays this lifecycle: at every stage we must know what dataset we are handling, where it came from, who is allowed to use it, and how it has been transformed. This is what allows you to re-run a backtest from three years ago, respond confidently to an audit, or debug a subtle failure in a live trading agent.

Right after this high-level overview, it is helpful to visualize the pipeline we will keep referring to.

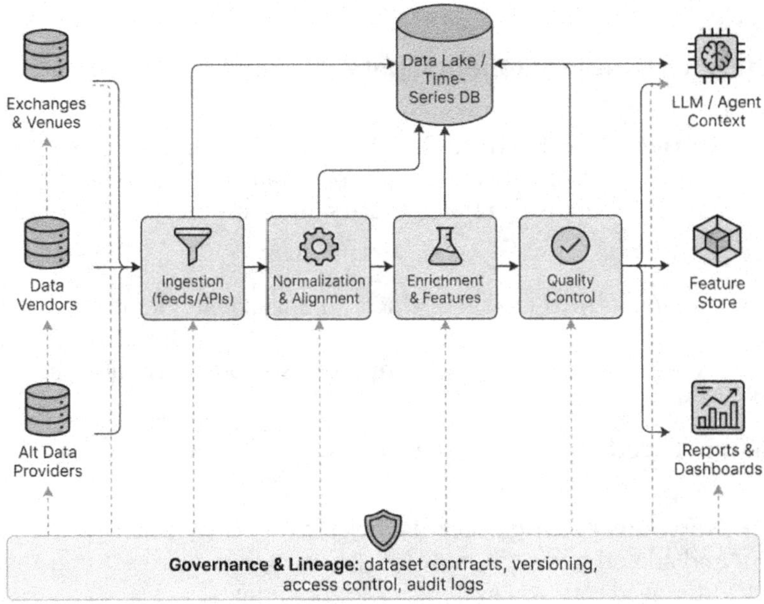

Market Data Sources and Modalities

Market data comes in many forms. Understanding these modalities is the first step toward coherent pipeline design.

Core price and volume data.

- **Ticks**: individual trades and quotes at specific timestamps. These are granular and large, used for microstructure research, execution algorithms, and intraday agents.
- **Bars**: aggregated over fixed intervals (for example, 1-minute OHLCV). Bars compress ticks into manageable time series, and form the backbone of many factor and forecasting models.
- **Order books**: snapshots or event streams of the limit order book. Critical for execution and market-making agents, but heavy and sensitive to time alignment.

Reference and fundamental data.

- **Static reference data**: identifiers, listing venues, corporate actions, sector classifications. These data ensure that a symbol today can be correctly related to the same economic entity five years ago.
- **Fundamental and risk data**: financial statements, analyst estimates, credit ratings, risk model exposures. These are typically lower frequency but crucial for cross-sectional ML models.

Unstructured and alternative data.

- **News and filings**: textual streams with timestamps, issuers, and sometimes sentiment labels. In a generative setting, these often feed retrieval systems or LLM contexts.
- **Alternative data**: web traffic, satellite imagery, card transaction aggregates, ESG scores, and more. These often have their own licensing, latency, and quality characteristics.

Each of these types has distinct *shape* (row size, frequency, schema) and *constraints* (licensing, entitlement, retention). A well-designed pipeline respects those differences while still converging them into a coherent downstream representation that your models can rely on.

Ingestion: Getting Data into Your House

Ingestion is the process of moving data from external (or upstream internal) sources into your controlled environment. For most financial firms, ingestion comes in three main flavors: batch, micro-batch, and streaming.

Batch ingestion. Vendors deliver daily files, often with trade or quote data for the previous session, plus updated reference data. Batch ingestion jobs run on a schedule (for example, nightly after the market close), check that the files are present and complete, parse them into a structured format, and land them into a raw zone in your data lake.

Micro-batch ingestion. For intraday research and many agentic applications, waiting until the end of the day is too slow. Micro-batching processes small chunks of data at frequent intervals (every few minutes or seconds). This strikes a balance between full streaming and simple batch: you can still use many "batch-like" tools while keeping latency reasonably low.

Streaming ingestion. Execution algorithms, market-making systems, and some real-time monitoring agents require streaming. Here, data arrives continuously over message buses or streaming platforms. The ingestion layer validates and persists data as it arrives, often with more complex logic to handle out-of-order messages and temporary network issues.

Across all three modes, the ingestion design should emphasize:

- **Idempotency**: re-running an ingestion job with the same input should not corrupt or duplicate data. This is important when you need to backfill or recover from failures.

- **Schema enforcement**: validating field types, required columns, and basic sanity checks (for example, price $>$ 0). Reject or quarantine bad records early.

- **Initial lineage capture**: attach metadata such as source system, file name, delivery time, and vendor version. This forms the start of the data's traceable history.

Normalization and Alignment

Once raw data is safely ingested, the next task is to make it consistent. Different vendors will disagree on symbol formats, time conventions, and even corporate action treatments. Normalization and alignment aim to remove these inconsistencies.

Common schemas and identifiers. Decide on canonical fields for core entities such as instruments, venues, and calendars. For example, you might map multiple vendor tickers to a single internal instrument ID, and enforce that all downstream data uses this ID. Reference data tables become the "dictionary" that connects external codes to internal ones.

Time zones and calendars. Markets operate on different time zones and trading calendars. Normalize timestamps to a consistent reference (often UTC), but also attach the local market time and the appropriate trading calendar. For time series, this makes it possible to line up events across regions and assets.

Corporate actions and prices. Corporate actions such as splits and dividends need to be handled in a consistent way. Many pipelines store both raw and adjusted prices, with clear labels on which is which. Downstream ML models can then select the appropriate series depending on the task (for example, forecasting raw vs. adjusted returns).

The goal of this stage is that, once data has passed through normalization, any two datasets that refer to the same asset and time can be safely joined and compared. This is critical for multi-source features and for LLM-based retrieval, where you may need to assemble a consistent context from prices, news, and fundamentals.

Enrichment and Feature Construction

Enrichment is where we start to turn raw financial data into inputs that models and agents can use directly. This includes both simple derived fields and richer features or labels.

Derived fields. Simple transformations such as returns, spreads, and volatility estimates are usually implemented as reusable building blocks. For example:

- Log returns over various horizons.
- Bid-ask spreads and mid-prices from quote data.
- Rolling volume and volatility estimates.

These transformations should be defined in a central place (for example, a data transformation library) and applied consistently, rather than reimplemented ad hoc in each research notebook.

Joins and cross-sectional information. Many useful features arise from joining across datasets: combining prices with sector classifications, fundamentals, or risk exposures. The earlier normalization of identifiers and time zones makes these joins tractable and less error-prone.

Event and label construction. Supervised learning and reinforcement learning often rely on labels that describe what happened after some decision point. For example, you might label each day with the next-day return, or label each trade with whether it was followed by a price improvement. Constructing these labels is a form of enrichment that should itself be part of the pipeline, with versions and metadata, not an informal step in a researcher's code.

Enrichment is a natural place to integrate *feature stores*, which we will discuss later in the chapter. For now, the key idea is that features and labels should be computed in a reproducible, shareable way, and not rediscovered from scratch in every project.

Quality Control: Making Data Trustworthy

Quality control is the immune system of your data platform. Its job is to detect and mitigate problems early enough that they do not infect models or trading decisions.

Typical checks include:

- **Completeness checks**: have we received data for all expected instruments, markets, and time intervals? Are there suspicious gaps?

- **Validity checks**: are fields within expected ranges (for example, prices non-negative, volumes not absurdly large)? Are timestamps monotonic where they should be?
- **Consistency checks**: do total volumes in intraday data roughly match end-of-day aggregates? Do corporate actions align with vendor-supplied calendars?
- **Statistical anomaly detection**: has the distribution of a feature changed abruptly in a way that likely indicates a data issue (for example, all prices for a market suddenly exactly equal)?

When a quality check fails, you need defined responses:

- Quarantine the affected data (for example, placing it into a "bad" zone).
- Raise alerts to data engineering or vendor management teams.
- Optionally, apply automated corrections when they are safe and well-understood (for example, filling isolated missing ticks with the last known price, but only under certain conditions).

For agentic systems and LLM-based workflows, quality control should extend beyond numeric anomalies. Textual feeds might have encoding issues, missing fields, or sudden changes in formatting that break parsers. Monitoring parsers and extractors for error rates becomes part of quality assurance.

Storage Architectures: Latency, Cost, and Regulation

Once data is clean and enriched, it needs to live somewhere that supports both heavy research workloads and low-latency operations. A typical financial data platform blends several storage patterns:

Data lakes. Large, relatively inexpensive object stores for raw and curated data. They hold tick history, reference data, and intermediate tables. They are ideal for backfills, historical research, and offline model training.

Columnar stores and warehouses. Systems optimized for analytical queries over large tables (for example, reading hundreds of columns across millions of rows). These are useful for factor research, risk analysis, and dashboards.

Time-series databases. Specialized stores for high-volume time series with efficient time-based queries. Useful for intraday monitoring, signal computation, and execution analytics.

Caches and key-value stores. For ultra-low-latency needs (for example, live execution agents or near-real-time LLM context assembly), precomputed features or recent state may be cached closer to the application.

Regulation and contracts often dictate where data may be stored, for how long, and who may access it. Some vendors restrict data to specific regions or require proof of deletion after license termination. Your storage design must be able to enforce these policies, which connects directly to governance and entitlements.

Governance, Lineage, and Auditability

Everything described so far will fail in a regulated setting without a governance layer. Governance is not just an access control list; it is an organized system of rules and metadata that makes your data understandable, trustworthy, and compliant.

Dataset contracts and catalogs. Each dataset in your platform should have a contract: a description of its schema, semantics, refresh cadence, quality expectations, and entitlements. A centralized catalog stores these contracts and lets users discover what data exists and how it may be used. For generative systems, this catalog can be exposed to agents as a "tooling map" of available datasets.

Lineage tracking. Lineage answers the question: "given this table, feature, or model input, what upstream data and transformations produced it?" Practically, this means recording for each dataset:

- Its direct sources (for example, which raw vendor files or upstream tables).
- The transformation logic or job that produced it (for example, a

specific version of an enrichment script).

- The time and environment in which it was produced.

Modern data orchestration tools can often capture lineage automatically, but the conceptual requirement is simple: you must be able to move backward from any derived artifact to its roots. This is essential for explaining model behavior to risk managers or regulators.

Versioning and reproducibility. Financial data changes over time, not just in content but in definition: vendors adjust historical records, corporate actions are restated, classification schemas evolve. To reproduce a backtest from two years ago, you need to know *which* version of the data it used.

Common practices include:

- **Snapshotting**: storing immutable snapshots of key datasets at regular intervals or when used by important experiments.
- **Time-travel**: using storage technologies that allow querying a dataset "as of" a previous point in time.
- **Experiment metadata**: for each model run or backtest, storing references to the exact data versions and transformation code that were used.

For generative agents, this level of reproducibility is equally important: if an LLM-based research assistant produced a recommendation or report on a particular date, you should be able to reconstruct the context that was available at that time.

Access control and entitlements. Not everyone is allowed to see every dataset. Licenses, privacy rules, and internal policies require fine-grained entitlements: which users, groups, or systems may access which data, for what purpose.

A governance layer typically:

- Enforces access at query time, based on the requesting identity and purpose.

- Maintains an audit log of access events: who queried what, when, and from where.
- Integrates with upstream license definitions to prevent unauthorized usage (for example, preventing a dataset licensed only for risk management from being used in a client-facing product).

For agentic systems, remember that agents act on behalf of users. An agent that composes a query or constructs an LLM context must inherit its user's entitlements. The data platform should ensure that, even when the agent is creative, it cannot assemble a context from data the user is not allowed to see.

Audit trails. Regulators and internal control functions will occasionally ask: "How did you arrive at this trade, recommendation, or model decision?" Audit trails tie together data access logs, lineage, and model metadata so that you can reconstruct the chain of events.

In practice, this often means:

- Logging the inputs and outputs of key models or agents (in a privacy- and license-aware way).
- Storing references to the exact datasets and versions involved in each decision.
- Ensuring that logs themselves are tamper-evident and retained for the required period.

From Pipelines to Agentic Workflows

With robust pipelines and governance in place, you can safely layer more advanced ML and generative components on top. Supervised and unsupervised models will draw from the enriched and validated feature sets. Reinforcement learning agents will rely on accurately simulated or historical environments built from your time-series stores. LLM-based agents will exploit the catalog and storage layers via retrieval tools, pulling licensed, clean data into prompts or tool chains.

The central message is that generative AI for finance does not start with prompts or models; it starts with trustworthy data. An end-to-end pipeline, anchored in governance and lineage, is what turns raw market feeds into a foundation on which you can confidently build research systems, trading strategies, and agentic workflows that can withstand both market stress and regulatory scrutiny.

2.2 Compute Infrastructure and Performance Engineering

The previous section focused on building trustworthy data pipelines and governance. Once that foundation is in place, the next constraint is no longer "Do we have the right data?" but "Can we process it fast enough, reliably enough, and cheaply enough to support our research and trading workflows?"

This section is about that machinery. We will:

- Map common financial AI workloads to appropriate compute patterns.
- Discuss hardware choices, especially when GPUs and accelerators are genuinely useful.
- Introduce cloud-native architectures that keep your system elastic and maintainable.
- Explore performance techniques for both training and inference.
- Highlight observability and cost control as first-class engineering goals.

Throughout, keep in mind that our eventual consumers are not just batch risk reports or offline backtests, but also agentic systems and generative models that interact with markets and humans in real time. They impose stricter requirements on latency, availability, and explainability of performance behavior.

From Data Pipelines to Compute Workloads

Well-governed data unlocks a spectrum of workloads in a typical quant or trading organization. It is useful to group these by their performance and infrastructure profile.

ETL and feature pipelines. These jobs take raw or lightly processed data from your pipelines and transform it into analysis-ready datasets or feature tables. They are usually:

- High volume (many symbols, long histories).
- Moderately latency-sensitive (minutes to hours, depending on frequency).
- Highly parallelizable across time, assets, or instruments.

Backtests and simulations. Strategy backtests, factor research, and Monte Carlo simulations consume large historical datasets and simulate trading or risk scenarios. They are:

- Bursty: demand spikes when research intensifies, then falls.
- Compute-heavy: many paths, many strategies, or both.
- Often embarrassingly parallel: different parameter sets or random seeds can run independently.

Model training. This includes:

- Classic ML (tree-based models, linear models, time-series models).
- Deep learning (sequence models for prices, transformers for text, LLM fine-tuning).
- Reinforcement learning (policy training, environment simulations).

Training is typically the strongest candidate for specialized hardware and distributed computing, especially as models grow in size or as you add more assets and features.

Inference and live scoring. Inference workloads appear in:

- Intraday signal computation and alpha scoring.
- Execution algorithms that adapt to order book state.
- LLM- and tool-based agents answering queries, monitoring markets, or recommending trades.

Here latency and availability are crucial. A 50 ms delay can be irrelevant for long-horizon portfolio construction but unacceptable for a market-making or smart order routing agent.

Recognizing these workload types makes it easier to reason about infrastructure: not everything needs a GPU cluster, not everything must be sub-millisecond, and not everything warrants a Kubernetes deployment.

Cloud-Native Building Blocks

Modern financial AI infrastructure is overwhelmingly cloud-oriented, even at firms with significant on-premise estates. "Cloud-native" here means designing systems to exploit elasticity, managed services, and automation rather than simply lifting and shifting monolithic applications.

Key architectural ideas include:

Separation of concerns. Data storage, compute, and orchestration are distinct layers:

- Storage: data lakes, warehouses, time-series stores as discussed previously.
- Compute: fleets of machines or containers that run ETL jobs, training runs, and services.

- Orchestration: schedulers and workflow engines that coordinate jobs and manage dependencies.

This separation lets you evolve each layer independently-for example, upgrading compute hardware without rewriting your data layer.

Containerization and microservices. Packaging applications (training scripts, feature jobs, inference services) into containers achieves:

- Environment consistency between development and production.
- Easier scaling and placement across clusters.
- Clear boundaries for resource allocation and security.

Microservices are small, focused services (for example, "LLM scoring API," "order book feature service," "risk aggregation service") that can scale and be deployed independently. Not every component must be a microservice, but decomposing large systems into sensible units improves agility and reliability.

Orchestration and workflow management. Tools like workflow managers and job schedulers allow you to express dependencies between tasks (for example, "after today's ETL finishes, run the daily alpha pipeline, then trigger model scoring"). They provide:

- Retry and failure handling.
- Logging and audit trails.
- Integration with resource managers (for example, spinning up ephemeral clusters for heavy jobs).

This orchestration layer is where you connect the end of your data pipelines to the start of your ML and agentic workloads.

Hardware Choices: CPUs, GPUs, and Beyond

A central question for finance teams is when to pay for specialized accelerators instead of general-purpose CPUs. The answer depends heavily on workload characteristics.

CPUs: the default workhorse. CPUs excel at:

- ETL and feature engineering with rich I/O and branching logic.
- Traditional quant workloads (backtests, Monte Carlo) that are easy to parallelize over many CPU cores.
- Light-weight model training and scoring (linear models, tree ensembles, simple time-series models).

In many shops, the majority of daily compute still happens on CPU-based clusters, especially for tasks where data movement and complex control flow overshadow numerical heavy lifting.

GPUs: high throughput for the right tasks. GPUs shine when:

- The same mathematical operations are applied to large batches of data (for example, matrix multiplications in deep learning).
- You train or fine-tune large models (LLMs, deep sequence models) where floating-point operations dominate.
- You need to accelerate inference for large models under latency or throughput constraints.

However, GPUs are more expensive and sometimes underutilized if workloads are sporadic or poorly batched. In finance, it is common to see:

- CPU clusters handling most ETL, backtests, and classical ML.
- Smaller GPU pools dedicated to deep learning and LLM experiments.
- Production GPU services for specific high-value models (for example, a central LLM agent or a critical execution policy).

Hybrid and heterogeneous clusters. In practice, you will combine CPU and GPU resources. Some patterns:

- **Hybrid training pipelines**: CPUs perform heavy preprocessing and data loading; GPUs handle model updates.
- **Multi-tier inference**: a CPU-based model handles most requests, escalating only complex or ambiguous cases to a GPU-based LLM.
- **Burst GPU usage**: on-demand GPU instances are acquired only when certain jobs run (for example, monthly LLM fine-tuning), keeping steady-state costs low.

The key is to match resource types to workload profiles deliberately, rather than defaulting to "everything on GPU" or "everything on CPU."

Performance Engineering for Training

Once you have chosen your hardware, the next challenge is to use it efficiently. For training workloads this means:

Parallelism strategies. Large training jobs often require multiple machines and devices. Three common approaches are:

- **Data parallelism**: different workers process different mini-batches of data and periodically synchronize model updates. This is usually the first and simplest step to scale training.
- **Model parallelism**: a single model is split across multiple devices because it does not fit into the memory of one. This is more complex but necessary for very large models.
- **Pipeline parallelism**: different layers or blocks of the model run on different devices, with data flowing through them like an assembly line.

Financial workloads often combine moderate model sizes with large datasets. In that case, data parallelism across many GPUs or CPUs can yield substantial speedups without extreme complexity.

Mixed precision and numerical considerations. Many modern accelerators can process lower-precision numbers (for example, 16-bit floats) significantly faster than 32-bit ones. For deep learning models that are robust to small numerical noise, mixed-precision training can:

- Reduce memory usage, allowing larger batch sizes or models.
- Speed up training significantly on supported hardware.

You must still validate that numerical stability and model quality remain acceptable, especially for sensitive risk or pricing applications.

Efficient data pipelines during training. Training can stall not because the model is slow, but because data loading and preprocessing cannot keep up. To avoid this:

- Precompute expensive features where possible and store them in accessible formats.
- Use parallel data loaders that overlap I/O and computation.
- Place training data in storage close to the compute (for example, in the same region or even on local SSDs).

These considerations link back to the earlier data engineering section: performance-conscious feature pipelines and storage formats (columnar, compressed, partitioned) pay off directly in faster training runs.

Checkpointing and fault tolerance. Training large models can take hours or days. Failures are inevitable due to hardware, network, or software issues. Robust training infrastructure:

- Saves model checkpoints periodically (for example, after each epoch or fixed number of steps).
- Logs training metrics and hyperparameters centrally.
- Supports resuming from the latest checkpoint with minimal manual intervention.

This is not just a convenience; in regulated environments, reproducible training runs and traceable model evolution are part of governance.

Performance Engineering for Inference

Inference is where many generative and agentic applications face their hardest constraints. A research backtest can tolerate a 10% slowdown; a live order execution agent or a conversational research assistant might not.

Latency versus throughput. Two core metrics must often be balanced:

- **Latency**: how long a single request takes from input to output.
- **Throughput**: how many requests can be processed per unit time.

For trading agents, latency directly impacts execution quality or responsiveness. For batch reporting or overnight scoring, throughput matters more than latency for any single request.

Techniques differ depending on which metric you prioritize. For example, batching multiple requests together can improve throughput on GPUs but may increase latency for individual requests.

Model size and quantization. Large models are powerful but costly to run. Inference optimization strategies include:

- **Model distillation**: training smaller "student" models to mimic larger "teacher" models, capturing most of their behavior at lower cost.
- **Quantization**: reducing the numerical precision of model weights and activations at inference time, often to 8-bit integers, which can speed up computation and reduce memory footprint with modest impact on accuracy.
- **Model specialization**: training domain-specific variants (for example, an LLM specialized for earnings calls) that are smaller but perform well on the targeted tasks.

For finance, where every basis point matters, you must empirically validate that these optimizations preserve the economic quality of outputs, not only raw prediction metrics.

Serving architectures. Inference services are typically deployed as:

- Stateless microservices exposing APIs (for example, REST or gRPC).
- Behind load balancers that distribute requests across replicas.
- With auto-scaling policies based on observed load (for example, CPU/GPU utilization, request queue length, or error rates).

Agentic systems complicate this picture because a single user interaction may trigger multiple model calls and tool invocations. Designing for this means:

- Caching intermediate results (for example, embeddings for frequently queried documents, or recent feature vectors for active instruments).
- Prioritizing requests based on context (for example, live trading-related calls have higher priority than exploratory research queries).
- Setting sensible timeouts and fallbacks (for example, degrade from an LLM-based explanation to a precomputed template if latency spikes).

Observability and Reliability as Performance Features

A compute platform cannot be tuned or trusted without observability: the ability to see what is happening across your infrastructure, in real time and historically.

Metrics, logs, and traces. Effective observability combines:

- **Metrics**: numerical time series such as CPU/GPU utilization, memory usage, request latency, error rates, and queue sizes.
- **Logs**: textual records of events, warnings, and errors from services and jobs.

- **Traces**: request-level timelines that show how a single call flows through multiple services or components.

For ML and generative workloads, it is helpful to add *model-aware* metrics: prediction distributions, drift indicators, or LLM token usage per request. This helps disentangle model issues from infrastructure issues.

SLOs and guardrails. Service-level objectives (SLOs) define acceptable performance and availability targets-for example, "99% of inference requests for the execution agent respond within 50 ms" or "daily ETL completes before 6:00 a.m. on trading days."

Guardrails enforce these objectives and protect the rest of the system when something goes wrong. Examples include:

- Circuit breakers that stop sending traffic to a failing service and trigger fallbacks.
- Budget limits for cloud resource usage, coupled with alerts when spending exceeds thresholds.
- Rate limits on certain classes of requests (for example, capping heavy LLM usage from non-critical tools).

Agentic systems bring new kinds of risk: an autonomous agent might inadvertently trigger expensive or redundant computations. Designing SLOs and guardrails that constrain agent behavior at the infrastructure level is just as important as constraining it at the prompt or policy level.

Cost-Aware Engineering

Finally, financial firms are acutely sensitive to costs. Compute and storage bills are another form of P&L, and must be managed with the same discipline.

Right-sizing and autoscaling. Avoid running large clusters at low utilization:

- For bursty workloads (backtests, experiments), use ephemeral clusters or on-demand instances that spin up when needed and tear down after.

- For steady workloads (daily ETL, baseline scoring), consider reserved or committed-use instances to reduce unit costs.
- Configure autoscaling policies that respond to genuine load rather than transient spikes.

Spot and preemptible instances. Many cloud providers offer discounted instances that can be reclaimed on short notice. These are well-suited to:

- Fault-tolerant training jobs with robust checkpointing.
- Large-scale simulations where losing some progress is acceptable.

They are less appropriate for latency-critical inference or stateful services.

Profiling and efficiency. Cost control is not only about instance choice; it is also about software efficiency:

- Profile code paths to identify hotspots and unnecessary computations.
- Reuse results where possible (for example, precompute embeddings or features instead of recomputing them in every agent call).
- Retire unused models, services, and pipelines that still consume resources out of habit.

Aligning incentives. Engineering and research teams should have visibility into the cost impact of their workloads. Simple dashboards that show "cost per training run" or "cost per thousand agent interactions" help make trade-offs explicit and encourage more efficient designs.

Bringing It Together for Agentic and Generative Systems

A robust compute infrastructure turns the data pipelines from the previous section into living systems: ETL jobs populate fresh features; training jobs explore new models; inference services respond to queries from traders, quants, and autonomous agents.

For agentic workflows, three themes recur:

- **Elasticity**: the ability to scale up when markets are volatile or research demand spikes, and to scale down when calm returns.
- **Latency management**: carefully matching model complexity and deployment choices to the time horizon of decisions.
- **Governed performance**: embedding observability, guardrails, and cost-awareness so that powerful agents operate within safe technical and financial bounds.

With these compute and performance foundations in place, we can now turn to the modeling layer itself: supervised and unsupervised learning methods that will consume the curated data and run atop the infrastructure described here, forming the analytic core that generative and reinforcement learning components will later orchestrate.

2.3 Supervised & Unsupervised Learning Foundations

With data pipelines and compute infrastructure in place, we can now turn to the models that will sit on top of them. This section builds the core machine learning (ML) toolkit for financial applications. Our goal is not to catalog every algorithm, but to give you a clear, structured view of:

- How to frame financial problems as *supervised* or *unsupervised* learning tasks.

- How to design feature pipelines that are reproducible and compatible with the data engineering foundations you have just seen.
- How to evaluate models in a way that survives regime shifts and supports later generative and agentic systems.

We will work mainly with time-series and panel data, because that is what most trading and risk systems see every day. Along the way, keep in mind that the same concepts will later apply when LLMs call these models as tools, or when generative components produce features, labels, or synthetic scenarios.

Supervised Learning in Financial Contexts

Supervised learning is about learning a mapping from inputs (features) to outputs (labels) when you already know the correct answers from historical data. In finance, "labels" are often future outcomes or categories you care about, such as:

- Next-period return of a stock or portfolio.
- Probability of default for a bond or counterparty.
- Whether a transaction is fraudulent.
- Whether a piece of text (an earnings call, news article, or chat) is positive, negative, or neutral for a given asset.

Structuring data into samples, features, and labels.

The first step is to turn your cleaned datasets into a table where each row is a *sample* and each column is either a feature or a label. For a daily stock-return prediction task, a sample might be:

- **Sample index**: (stock ID, date).
- **Features**: past returns, volatility, fundamentals, sector information, sentiment scores.
- **Label**: next-day return or an indicator of whether the stock outperforms a benchmark.

Two principles are crucial in finance:

- **Temporal order**: features must use information available *at or before* the time of the decision. You cannot use tomorrow's earnings surprise to predict today's price.
- **Granularity and alignment**: features from different sources (prices, fundamentals, news) must be aligned in time and instrument space, using the normalization and enrichment steps from the data pipelines section.

Your earlier investment in consistent time zones, calendars, and identifiers now pays off: supervised datasets are simply structured views of your curated data lake.

Common supervised tasks in finance.

- **Return forecasting.** Predicting the sign or magnitude of future returns over horizons from minutes to months. Labels might be raw returns, excess returns over a benchmark, or binary "up vs. down" indicators.
- **Risk and default modeling.** Estimating credit risk, loss given default, or Value-at-Risk. Targets can be binary (default vs. non-default) or continuous (loss amount, volatility).
- **Anomaly and fraud detection.** Classifying transactions or orders as normal or suspicious. Often there are few positive examples, which affects model choice and evaluation.
- **Document and event classification.** Assigning categories or sentiment to news, filings, and calls. These tasks often combine classic supervised methods with embeddings from pre-trained language models or LLMs.

The algorithms themselves range from linear models and gradient-boosted trees to deep networks. What matters for this chapter is understanding how to structure the problem and data so that any chosen algorithm can be applied correctly.

Avoiding information leakage.

Information leakage occurs when your training data includes hints about the future that would not be available at prediction time. In finance, leakage is common and dangerous, because it can produce extremely impressive backtest results that evaporate in live trading.

Sources of leakage include:

- Using post-event prices or fundamentals to construct past features.
- Joining datasets using future knowledge (for example, sector classifications that were revised later).
- Randomly shuffling time series in cross-validation, which mixes past and future.

Defensive strategies:

- Always reason explicitly about the "information set" available at each timestamp.
- Use lagged features (for example, yesterday's close, last quarter's earnings) instead of contemporaneous values that may be revised.
- Use time-aware validation schemes (walk-forward, rolling windows) rather than standard random splits.

Later, when LLM-based agents orchestrate workflows, they depend on these guardrails: if the base supervised models are leakage-prone, the agent's higher-level reasoning will still rest on sand.

Unsupervised Learning for Structure Discovery

Unsupervised learning deals with data where no explicit labels are given. Instead of predicting a known outcome, we try to discover patterns, clusters, or compressed representations.

In finance, unsupervised methods are workhorses for:

- Grouping similar instruments, clients, or behaviors.
- Compressing high-dimensional features into a smaller set of factors.
- Detecting outliers without a labeled "fraud" or "anomaly" class.

Clustering.

Clustering algorithms try to partition data points into groups such that points in the same group are more similar to each other than to those in other groups. Examples include:

- Grouping stocks by return patterns, leading to empirical "sectors" or risk clusters.
- Segmenting clients by trading or investment behavior, to tailor products or risk limits.

The key design decision is the *feature space* in which clustering is performed. If you cluster on raw prices, you will get different results than if you cluster on normalized returns, factor exposures, or risk measures. This again emphasizes the importance of thoughtful feature engineering.

Dimensionality reduction and embeddings.

Many financial datasets have more features than are convenient to reason about directly. Dimensionality reduction techniques provide lower-dimensional representations that capture the main structure:

- Principal component analysis (PCA) on yield curves or factor returns produces a small number of "principal components" that explain most of the variance.
- Autoencoders or other deep embedding models learn compressed representations of instruments, clients, or documents.

These embeddings can then be used as inputs to supervised models, as similarity measures (for example, nearest neighbors), or as conditioning information for generative models. For example, a generative market simulator might be conditioned on a low-dimensional "market state" learned by an unsupervised model.

Anomaly detection without labels.

In some settings, you do not have clear labels for "bad" behavior, but you do know what "normal" looks like most of the time. Unsupervised or semi-supervised anomaly detection methods fit a model of normal behavior and then flag points that deviate strongly.

In finance, this can support:

- Market surveillance: detecting unusual trading patterns that may indicate manipulation.
- Operations monitoring: spotting abnormal delays, data gaps, or system failures.

Later, when we build agent-based monitors, these anomaly scores can be turned into triggers for alerts or deeper investigations by LLMs or human analysts.

Feature Engineering as a Process

Both supervised and unsupervised methods depend critically on features: the numerical or categorical representations of raw data that the algorithm can consume.

From raw time series to features.

For financial time series such as prices and volumes, common feature transformations include:

- Returns over different horizons (daily, weekly, intraday).
- Volatility estimates (rolling standard deviations, range-based measures).
- Volume and liquidity indicators (average daily volume, order book depth).

- Technical-style signals (moving averages, momentum indicators), used carefully and formally rather than as ad hoc heuristics.

For high-frequency or order book data:

- Relative depth at different price levels.
- Imbalance between bid and ask volumes.
- Short-term arrival rates of trades and orders.

For text and events:

- Bag-of-words or TF–IDF representations (for simpler models).
- Embeddings from pre-trained language models or finance-specific transformers.
- Structured event features: whether an earnings surprise occurred, whether guidance was raised or lowered.

The data pipelines you designed earlier should contain these transformations as reusable, versioned steps, not as one-off code fragments in notebooks.

Feature stores and transformation graphs.

A feature store is a central system that:

- Defines features and how they are computed.
- Stores historical values of features for model training.
- Serves up-to-date feature values for live inference.

Transformation graphs describe how features depend on raw inputs and on each other. This is essentially the ML-facing mirror of your data lineage system.

Benefits include:

- Reuse: the same feature definitions can be used by multiple models and teams.
- Consistency: training and inference use the *same* feature logic, reducing training-serving skew.
- Governance: each feature has an owner, documentation, and quality checks.

For generative systems, feature stores provide a clear, structured interface that agents can query: "give me all features available for stock X at time T" becomes a well-defined operation.

Evaluation and Validation in Time

Even the best algorithms and features are useless without rigorous evaluation. In finance, evaluation is made harder by three realities:

- Markets are non-stationary: distributions drift and regimes change.
- Data points are time-ordered and often autocorrelated.
- Backtests must respect trading frictions and microstructure.

Train/validation/test splits for time series.

Randomly shuffling data into train and test sets breaks temporal structure and invites leakage. Instead, we use time-aware splits, such as:

- **Holdout by time**: train on an early period, validate on a subsequent period, and test on a final, later period.
- **Walk-forward validation**: repeatedly train on a rolling window of history and evaluate on the immediately following period, then roll forward.

Walk-forward schemes mimic how the model would be used in practice: periodically retrained on the latest data, then applied to unseen future data.

Nested validation and hyperparameter tuning.

Hyperparameters (for example, tree depth, regularization strength, network width) should be tuned on validation sets that are separate from the final test period. This avoids overfitting your model selection process to the same data you use to report performance.

In time series, "nested" often means:

- An inner loop of walk-forward splits used to tune hyperparameters.
- An outer, untouched test period that evaluates the final chosen configuration.

This structure may sound complex, but orchestration tools and your compute infrastructure can automate much of it.

Realistic baselines and backtest hygiene.

A model that beats a naive baseline *in-sample* might still be useless after costs and slippage. Good evaluation includes:

- Comparing to simple rules: moving averages, cross-sectional mean reversion, buy-and-hold benchmarks.
- Including transaction costs, spreads, and market impact where appropriate.
- Respecting liquidity and execution constraints: you cannot trade infinite volume at the last traded price in illiquid names.

For generative and agentic systems, these baselines anchor expectations. If a sophisticated LLM-driven strategy cannot beat a well-tuned but simple supervised baseline after costs, you have learned something important.

Robustness and stability.

Finally, evaluation should explore robustness:

- Performance across different market regimes (bull, bear, high volatility).

- Sensitivity to small changes in hyperparameters or feature sets.
- Stability of feature importance or attributions over time.

These diagnostics are essential when models are subject to model risk governance and must be explained to human committees or regulators.

Recap: Supervised vs. Unsupervised Workflows

At this point, it is helpful to summarize and contrast how supervised and unsupervised learning fit into a financial time-series workflow. The following visual provides a side-by-side comparison.

This chart is intentionally simple numerically, but rich in annotations. It emphasizes that:

- Supervised methods optimize directly for predictive performance on labeled targets.
- Unsupervised methods optimize for compactness, separation, or density in feature space, producing structures that are often inputs to further models.

- Both share the same upstream feature pipelines and depend on the same evaluation discipline, but they answer different questions.

Preparing for Generative and Agentic Extensions

The concepts in this section form the "classical" ML substrate on which generative models and agentic systems will later operate:

- LLM-based agents will call supervised models as tools (for example, "risk_estimator" or "alpha_score") and will rely on their calibration and robustness.
- Generative models will often be conditioned on embeddings, factors, or regime labels that come from unsupervised learning.
- Evaluation frameworks developed here (walk-forward, cost-aware backtesting, robustness checks) will be reused to assess more complex agentic workflows.

By treating supervised and unsupervised learning as disciplined, well-governed components—rather than as ad hoc experiments—you create a modeling foundation that can safely support the more flexible, conversational, and autonomous systems that we will build in later chapters.

2.4 Reinforcement Learning Essentials

The previous sections have treated markets largely as sources of data for prediction and classification: given yesterday's information, what is the most likely outcome tomorrow? Reinforcement learning (RL) extends this picture. Instead of passively forecasting, an RL agent *acts* in an environment, receives feedback in the form of rewards, and learns a policy that maximizes long-run performance.

In trading and execution, this shift from prediction to sequential decision-making is crucial. A market-making algorithm must decide what quotes to post; an execution algorithm must schedule child orders over time; a portfolio agent must rebalance under constraints and costs. All of these are naturally sequential, state-dependent control problems, and RL provides a language and toolkit to reason about them.

This section introduces the core RL concepts tailored to financial markets: Markov Decision Processes (MDPs), policies, value functions, and exploration. We will connect them to concrete trading examples and highlight practical pitfalls you must keep in mind when later integrating RL into generative and agentic systems.

From Prediction to Sequential Decision-Making

Supervised learning asks: "Given features x, what is the label y?" There is no explicit notion of how one prediction influences the next. RL, in contrast, models a loop:

- The agent observes the current *state* of the environment.
- It chooses an *action*.
- The environment responds with a new state and a *reward*.
- The agent updates its strategy, trying to improve future rewards.

In a trading context:

- The **state** might include current prices, order book snapshots, your inventory, and time remaining in the day.
- The **action** might be to submit, modify, or cancel orders; or to change target allocations.
- The **reward** might be realized P&L, execution quality, or risk-adjusted performance.

Crucially, today's action affects tomorrow's state and opportunities. For example, an aggressive buy order may improve short-term execution but increase inventory risk. RL is built to capture this feedback.

Markov Decision Processes in Trading

The standard mathematical object behind RL is the Markov Decision Process (MDP). While we avoid heavy notation here, it is helpful to understand its components at an intuitive level:

- A set of **states** describing the environment at each decision point.
- A set of **actions** the agent can take.
- **Transition dynamics** describing how the environment moves from one state to another given an action.
- A **reward** signal quantifying immediate gain or loss from each transition.
- A **policy** describing how the agent chooses actions based on states.

States as market and inventory features.

In practice, "state" is always a vector of features extracted from your data pipelines. Examples:

- For an intraday execution agent: current mid-price, bid-ask spread, order book depth, time-of-day, remaining quantity to trade, and elapsed time since start.
- For a portfolio allocation agent: current holdings, risk factor exposures, recent returns and volatilities, available cash, and risk limits.

The Markov assumption says that this state representation captures all relevant information needed to make a good decision about the future. In finance, this is rarely perfectly true, but you can often construct a state that is "good enough" by including short histories or hidden variables relevant to your strategy.

Actions as trading or control decisions.

Actions depend heavily on the level at which you apply RL:

- At the *order* level: choosing limit prices, quantities, and order types (market, limit, iceberg).
- At the *execution schedule* level: deciding what fraction of a parent order to execute in each time bucket.
- At the *portfolio* level: adjusting target weights or exposures across assets or factors.

In all cases, actions should be defined so that they are implementable and respect constraints (position limits, regulatory rules, risk budgets). Later, when we integrate RL with LLM-based orchestration, those constraints will also be enforced at the agent-planning layer.

Rewards as economic objectives.

Rewards quantify how "good" an outcome is from the agent's perspective. Choosing a reward is as much a business decision as a technical one. Examples:

- For market making: incremental P&L minus an inventory penalty, to discourage unbalanced positions.
- For execution: negative implementation shortfall (that is, smaller shortfall leads to higher reward), or negative slippage relative to a benchmark such as VWAP.
- For portfolio allocation: risk-adjusted returns over a horizon, possibly including penalties for transaction costs or constraint violations.

Rewards can be immediate (per step), terminal (only at the end of an episode), or a mixture. For example, an intraday execution agent may receive small step rewards related to realized execution and a final reward based on total shortfall.

Policies: How an Agent Behaves

A *policy* is the agent's strategy: a mapping from states to actions. In simple cases, it can be a lookup table; in realistic markets, it is typically a parametric function (for example, a neural network) that outputs an action or a distribution over actions.

Deterministic vs. stochastic policies.

- A **deterministic policy** always picks the same action for a given state (for example, "if spread is small and inventory is long, place a sell order at price X").
- A **stochastic policy** defines probabilities over actions (for example, "with 70% probability place a moderately aggressive order, with 30% probability a more passive one").

Stochastic policies are useful for exploration and for modeling mixed strategies. In noisy markets, they also help prevent the agent from overfitting to specific patterns in historical data.

Policy parameterization and learning.

In practice, we represent a policy by a model with parameters θ (for example, the weights of a neural network). RL algorithms then try to adjust θ so as to maximize expected cumulative reward over time.

For a trading agent, you might:

- Feed in features such as prices, inventory, and time.
- Have the policy network output continuous actions (for example, target price offsets, order sizes) or discrete actions (for example, "buy," "sell," "hold").
- Train θ on historical or simulated episodes so that good sequences of actions become more likely under the policy.

Later, these policies can be wrapped as tools that higher-level LLM agents can call, for example: "execute this order using the EQ_EXECUTION_POLICY tool with current state features."

Value Functions: Looking Beyond the Next Tick

While rewards are instantaneous, trading performance is inherently cumulative. A single decision may have long-run consequences: taking on inventory now could yield profit or loss later depending on how the market moves.

Value functions quantify expected future reward from a given state or state-action pair under a particular policy. Intuitively:

- The **state-value** of s under policy π is the expected sum of rewards you will get from now on, if you start in s and follow π.
- The **action-value** (or Q-value) of (s, a) under π is the expected sum of rewards if you start in s, take action a once, and then follow π.

In trading terms:

- The state-value tells you how promising the current market and inventory configuration is, given your usual behavior.
- The action-value compares concrete choices (for example, whether to cross the spread now or wait) in terms of their long-run P&L impact.

RL algorithms often revolve around estimating these value functions and then improving the policy by favoring actions with higher estimated Q-values.

Value-Based vs. Policy-Based Methods

There are two broad RL families that you will see repeatedly: value-based and policy-based methods. Understanding their roles helps you select suitable approaches for financial problems.

Value-based methods.

Value-based methods, such as Q-learning and its deep variants, focus on learning an approximation of the action-value function $Q(s, a)$. Once you have Q, you can derive a policy by, for example, choosing the action with the highest estimated value in each state.

These methods work well when:

- The action space is relatively small and discrete (for example, "buy," "sell," "hold," or a few levels of aggression).
- You want a conceptually simple approach and can tolerate some exploration in the environment.

In finance, deep Q-networks have been experimented with for tasks like market making and inventory control. However, instability and sensitivity to hyperparameters can be significant in noisy, non-stationary markets.

Policy-based methods.

Policy-based methods, such as policy gradient algorithms, directly optimize the parameters of the policy to maximize expected reward, without explicitly modeling $Q(s, a)$ for all actions. They are especially useful when:

- The action space is continuous (for example, continuous price or size adjustments).
- You need stochastic policies by design.

A portfolio agent that outputs continuous weight changes or execution agents that choose continuous price offsets are natural fits for policy-based RL.

Actor-critic methods.

Actor-critic algorithms combine both worlds:

- The **actor** is the policy model that chooses actions.
- The **critic** is a value function estimator (state or action value) that critiques the actor's choices and guides learning.

This architecture tends to be more sample-efficient and stable, which is particularly important when data is expensive or you cannot explore freely in live markets. Many modern RL methods for finance (including those used in simulators and offline RL) fall into this category.

Exploration vs. Exploitation in Markets

A defining challenge in RL is the exploration-exploitation trade-off:

- **Exploitation** means choosing the currently best-known action to maximize reward.
- **Exploration** means trying actions that might yield better long-term rewards, even if they look worse based on current knowledge.

In traditional RL benchmarks (games, robotics), you can often explore aggressively: try random moves, crash the robot in simulation, and so on. Finance is different:

- Bad exploration loses real money or creates regulatory risk.
- Some actions (for example, spoofing, layering) are illegal regardless of their "reward."

Safer exploration strategies.

Practical RL in finance relies heavily on safer exploration mechanisms, including:

- **Simulators**: use realistic market simulators calibrated to historical data to explore candidate policies offline. The agent can try many strategies without real capital at risk.
- **Historical replays**: run the policy on past data as if it were live, simulating what would have happened given the recorded order book and trades.
- **Conservative policies**: restrict actions to a pre-approved, human-designed envelope (for example, never exceeding certain participation rates, or never crossing risk limits).
- **Bandit-style exploration**: in some settings (for example, choosing between a small number of execution algos), use bandit algorithms that control regret and exploration tightly.

Later, when LLMs orchestrate RL policies as tools, they can also enforce additional constraints in natural language ("never increase this position beyond X% of daily volume," "do not place orders within Y ms of major scheduled announcements"), which are then translated into hard bounds at the policy layer.

Non-Stationarity, Delayed Rewards, and Other Pitfalls

Financial markets are not static board games. Their statistical properties change over time; liquidity regimes shift; participants adapt. Several RL-specific pitfalls deserve early emphasis.

Non-stationary environments.

Most RL theory assumes that transition dynamics and reward distributions do not change over time. Markets violate this every day. Consequences:

- Policies trained on one regime (for example, low volatility) may perform poorly in another (for example, crisis conditions).
- Value estimates become stale as underlying distributions drift.

Mitigation strategies parallel those in supervised learning:

- Use rolling training windows and retrain policies periodically.
- Include regime indicators or macro features in the state.
- Regularize and constrain policies to avoid extreme behaviors that are sensitive to small distribution shifts.

Delayed and sparse rewards.

Some financial objectives are only realized after long horizons. For example, the success of a long-term portfolio strategy may be clear only after months or years. Delayed rewards make credit assignment difficult: which decisions were responsible for good or bad outcomes?

In practice:

- For shorter-horizon tasks (execution, intraday trading), design step rewards that reflect incremental progress (for example, per-child-order slippage).
- For longer-horizon tasks, use intermediate proxies (factor exposures, realized risk) to provide more frequent learning signals.

Simulator-reality mismatch.

Because exploration in live markets is dangerous, you will rely heavily on simulators and historical backtests. But no simulator is perfect:

- Real participants may react to your strategy in ways the simulator does not capture.
- Market impact models may be simplistic or miscalibrated.

This "sim-to-real gap" must be acknowledged in both model risk management and engineering design. Practical measures include:

- Conservative deployment: start with small capital and limited scope, gradually expanding if live performance matches simulations.
- Human-in-the-loop controls: traders or risk managers monitor early deployments and maintain veto power.
- Ongoing monitoring: compare live reward distributions and state visitation patterns with those seen in training to detect drift.

These considerations echo the governance themes from earlier sections, now applied to RL.

Offline RL and Batch-Constrained Methods

In many financial institutions, you have large historical datasets but limited ability to interactively collect new data. Offline RL (also called batch RL) focuses on learning policies entirely from logged data without further exploration.

Why offline RL fits finance.

- You may have years of order flow and execution records from existing strategies.
- You cannot afford to "explore" widely in live markets.
- Regulatory and compliance constraints limit experimental behavior.

Offline RL methods try to:

- Avoid learning policies that take actions rarely or never seen in the historical data (where value estimates are unreliable).
- Correct for bias in logged data (for example, historical strategies may have had their own exploration or selection biases).

Batch-constrained and conservative approaches.

Many practical algorithms operate under explicit constraints, such as:

- Keeping the new policy close to the behavior policy that generated the data.
- Penalizing actions that fall outside the historical support.

For an execution agent, this might mean that, from historical logs of VWAP-style trades, you learn modest improvements in timing or order placement, without radically different behaviors that the data cannot support.

Positioning RL Within the Agentic Stack

Finally, it is helpful to see RL not as an isolated technology but as a component within a broader agentic system:

- **RL policies as tools.** Once trained, an RL policy can be wrapped as a callable tool that takes a state vector and returns an action or recommendation. Higher-level LLM agents can decide when and how to invoke it.

- **LLMs as orchestrators and critics.** LLMs can help interpret RL behavior ("why did the execution agent slow down here?"), summarize performance across episodes, or propose constraints and modifications to reward functions.
- **Shared data and evaluation foundations.** RL agents rely on the same curated data pipelines, feature stores, and evaluation frameworks described in earlier sections. Backtest hygiene, versioned datasets, and governance are as crucial for RL as for supervised models.

As we move into later chapters, we will combine these elements: supervised models to estimate short-term returns or risks, unsupervised methods to characterize regimes and market states, RL policies to make sequential trading or execution decisions, and generative agents to orchestrate and explain it all. The conceptual tools you have just seen—MDPs, policies, value functions, and exploration—are the vocabulary in which those more sophisticated systems will quietly think.

Chapter 3

Generative Models, Retrieval, and Knowledge Systems

Most practitioners see large language models as black boxes that 'talk in paragraphs.' In this chapter, we crack that box open and follow the full signal path: from tokens and attention, to embeddings and vector search, to prompts that reliably call tools, to RAG and knowledge graphs that keep your agents grounded in real financial data. By the end, you'll understand not just how each piece works, but how to compose them into a research and trading stack that is fast, auditable, and deeply domain-aware.

3.1 Transformer Architecture and Domain Adaptation

In the previous chapter we treated large language models as powerful but opaque tools—systems that could summarize research, extract events, or draft analyses when given the right instructions. In this section we look inside the box just enough to understand how these models actually process financial text, and what that implies for adapting them to your own workflows without retraining them from scratch.

Our goal is practical intuition, not full mathematical detail. By the end, you should be able to answer three concrete questions:

- How does a transformer model "see" a 10-K, an earnings call, or a news feed?
- Which parts of the architecture matter for financial tasks?
- How can I efficiently specialize a base model for my firm's use cases?

From Text to Tokens to Vectors

Transformers do not operate on words or characters directly. They operate on *tokens*: small units of text such as subwords, common word pieces, or sometimes single characters.

When you send an earnings-call paragraph to a model, the first thing that happens is:

1. **Tokenization.** The raw string is broken into tokens using a fixed vocabulary learned during pre-training. Rare or long words are decomposed into shorter pieces. For example:
   - "macroeconomic" $\rightarrow$ macro + economic
   - "EBITDA" might be a single token if it was common in the training data.
2. **Integer mapping.** Each token is mapped to an integer ID. A sequence of text becomes a sequence of integers.
3. **Embeddings.** Each integer ID is mapped to a learned vector (for example, of length 1,024). This creates a matrix of size (sequence length) $\times$ (embedding dimension).

You can think of the embedding step as placing each token into a high-dimensional "semantic space" where tokens with similar usage and meaning (e.g., "EPS" and "earnings per share") are placed near one another.

Positional Information: Order Matters

A bag-of-words model ignores order; transformers do not. The self-attention mechanism they use needs to know which token comes first, second, and so on.

To provide this, the model adds a *positional encoding* to each token embedding. Conceptually, you can think of this as tagging each token vector with its location in the sequence, so that:

- "guidance" at the start of a sentence,
- "guidance" at the end,
- and "guidance" in the middle

all have slightly different vectors, even though they share the same base embedding.

There are several ways to implement positional information (fixed sinusoidal patterns, learned position embeddings, rotary encodings), but for our purposes the key idea is simple: the model sees not just *what* token is present, but also *where* it appears. This is crucial for finance, where phrases like "we expect" or "we no longer expect" can change meaning based on local structure.

The Transformer Stack: Layers of Self-Attention

Once the model has embedded each token and added positional information, it feeds the sequence through a stack of identical *transformer blocks*. Each block refines the representation of every token based on its relationship to all others.

At a high level, one transformer block contains:

1. A **multi-head self-attention** sublayer;
2. A **feed-forward** sublayer (a small neural network applied to each position);
3. **Layer normalization** and **residual connections** that stabilize training and preserve information.

Each block takes a matrix of size (sequence length) × (hidden dimension) as input and returns another matrix of the same size. Stacking many blocks gives the model depth: higher layers capture more abstract relationships, such as "this sentence is about future guidance" or "this clause mentions a legal risk."

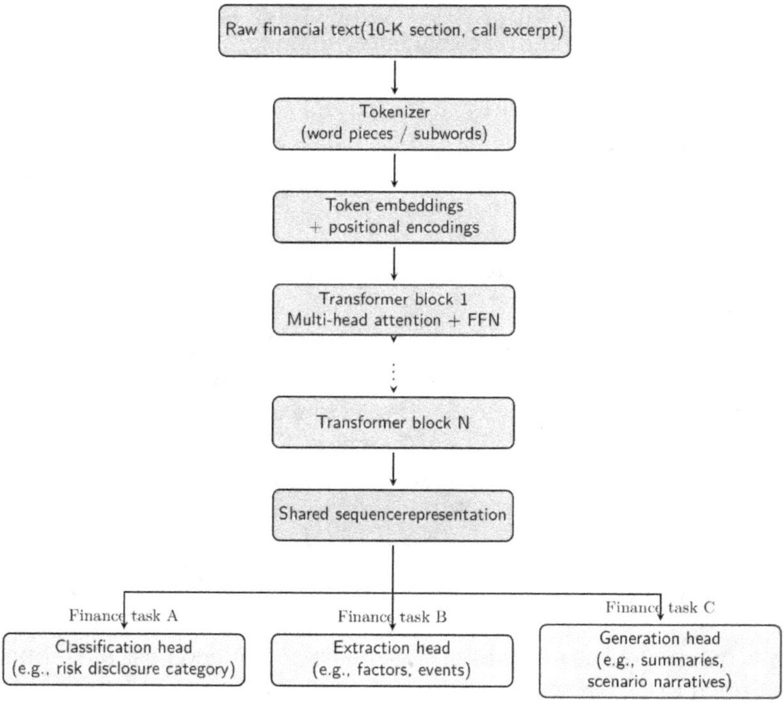

Self-Attention: Letting Every Token Look at Every Other

The core innovation of transformers is *self-attention*. In previous architectures like recurrent neural networks, each token was processed mostly in sequence; long-range relationships were hard to capture. Self-attention instead allows each token to directly "look at" all other tokens in the same sequence, regardless of distance.

Intuitively, for every word in an earnings call sentence, the model asks:

> Which other words in this paragraph are important for interpreting me?

For example, in the sentence:

> "We now expect full-year EPS to be at the lower end of the prior range due to weaker demand in Europe."

the token "lower" will attend strongly to "EPS", "full-year", and "prior range". The phrase "weaker demand in Europe" may link to tokens like "demand" and "Europe". The attention mechanism computes weights that express these relationships; higher weights mean stronger influence.

Multi-Head Attention: Multiple Views of the Same Sentence

In practice, a single pattern of attention is not enough. We want the model to capture different types of relationships at the same time:

- Syntactic relationships: which adjective modifies which noun.
- Temporal cues: words like "next quarter", "full-year", "historically".
- Financial semantics: words related to guidance, risk, liquidity, and so on.

Multi-head attention addresses this by running several attention mechanisms in parallel, each with its own parameters. Each "head" can specialize in a different kind of pattern. The outputs of all heads are then combined and passed on to the next layer.

You can think of multi-head attention as a small team of analysts looking at the same passage: one focuses on time references, one on risk language, one on numbers and units, and so forth. The model aggregates their perspectives into a richer representation.

Feed-Forward Layers and Residual Connections

After the attention step, each token's representation is passed through a small feed-forward network—essentially, a couple of linear transformations with a nonlinearity in between. This helps the model transform the attended information into more abstract features.

Residual connections add the original input of each sublayer back to its output. This can be viewed as saying:

> "Keep what we had from the previous layer, but add a refined correction computed by the current layer."

Layer normalization rescales activations to stay in a stable range, which is crucial when you stack dozens of layers.

The stack of transformer blocks therefore acts like a sequence of refinements:

- Lower layers capture local patterns (phrases, short dependencies).
- Mid layers capture sentence-level semantics (e.g., sentiment of a statement).
- Higher layers capture document-level context (e.g., the overall narrative around guidance or risk).

This layered structure is exactly what we want when working with long, nuanced financial documents.

Pre-Training Objectives: How the Model Learned Language

The transformer architecture is general; what makes a model powerful is how it was *pre-trained*. Two main families of objectives are widely used:

1. **Causal language modeling (CLM).** The model is trained to predict the next token given all previous tokens. This is the standard setup for generative models that complete or continue text.

They learn to model narratives, write coherent paragraphs, and reason step by step.

2. **Masked language modeling (MLM).** Some tokens are replaced with a special mask, and the model is trained to reconstruct the missing tokens using both left and right context. This is common in bidirectional models used for classification and extraction.

From a financial perspective:

- CLM-style models are well-suited for *generation* tasks: drafting earnings-call summaries, scenario narratives, analyst-style commentary.
- MLM-style models are strong at *understanding and labeling*: classifying risk disclosures, extracting events, tagging entities.

Modern systems often combine the strengths of both pre-training approaches, sometimes via additional training phases. For this chapter, it is enough to know that you typically start from a large, general-purpose model that has already learned a great deal of financial language indirectly, simply because financial text is prevalent in pre-training corpora.

Why Transformers Fit Financial Text

Transformers are particularly well matched to financial data for several reasons:

- **Long-range dependencies.** A risk mentioned in one section of a 10-K may only be resolved or quantified many paragraphs later. Self-attention can bridge these distances.
- **Noisy, redundant language.** Earnings calls often repeat and rephrase themes. Attention allows the model to aggregate signals across repeated mentions.

- **Heterogeneous structure.** Tables, bullet lists, boilerplate, and narrative all coexist in filings. Transformers can, in principle, attend across these structures without manually engineered features.

Understanding this fit clarifies why it makes sense to build research and trading agents on top of transformer-based models, and why investing in good adaptation strategies is worthwhile.

Domain Adaptation: From General Model to Financial Specialist

Training a transformer from scratch is almost never economical for a single firm. It requires billions of tokens and enormous compute budgets. Instead, you typically start with a strong base model and *adapt* it to your domain.

There are two broad strategies:

1. **Full fine-tuning:** updating all the model's parameters on your task-specific data.
2. **Parameter-efficient fine-tuning (PEFT):** freezing most of the model and only learning a small number of additional parameters.

The right choice depends on your data volume, latency and memory constraints, and how different your tasks are from general language modeling.

Full Fine-Tuning

In full fine-tuning, you take the entire pre-trained model and continue training it on your specific objective. Examples include:

- Classifying paragraphs of 10-Ks into detailed risk categories used by your internal rating system.

- Generating normalized, structured event descriptions (e.g., earnings surprises, guidance changes) for backtesting.

Advantages:

- Maximum flexibility: the entire network can adapt.
- Potentially highest accuracy if you have a very large, high-quality labeled dataset.

Disadvantages:

- Expensive in compute and memory; you must store a full copy of the model per variant.
- Higher risk of overfitting or degrading the base model's general abilities if not carefully managed.

For most financial teams, full fine-tuning of cutting-edge models is overkill. Parameter-efficient methods are usually more practical.

Adapters and LoRA: Parameter-Efficient Fine-Tuning

Parameter-efficient fine-tuning methods aim to capture domain-specific adjustments with far fewer parameters, while keeping the frozen base model intact. Two common approaches are:

Adapters. Small neural network modules are inserted into each transformer block (often after the feed-forward sublayer). During training, only these adapter parameters are updated; the original weights remain frozen.

You can think of adapters as "sidecar" layers that learn how to tweak the model's representation for your domain. Because adapters are small, you can maintain many domain-specific variants (e.g., one for credit risk, one for macro research) without storing multiple full models.

LoRA (Low-Rank Adaptation). Instead of adding full adapter layers, LoRA injects low-rank matrices into existing weight matrices, particularly in the attention and feed-forward parts of the model. These low-rank updates are much smaller than the original matrices but can still capture meaningful shifts in behavior.

From an engineering standpoint, LoRA has several attractive properties:

- Memory footprint is small compared to full fine-tuning.
- You can combine multiple LoRA adapters at inference time (for example, one capturing legal/regulatory nuances and another capturing sector-specific language).
- Switching between tasks is as simple as loading different LoRA weights on top of the same base model.

In both adapters and LoRA, the key idea is the same: reuse the heavy, general-purpose transformer stack, and learn thin, task-specific layers on top.

Choosing the Right Adaptation Strategy

How should a financial practitioner choose between these options? A few guiding questions:

- **How much labeled data do you have?**
  - If you have tens of thousands of well-labeled examples (e.g., paragraphs annotated with risk taxonomy labels), PEFT methods like adapters or LoRA are usually sufficient.
  - If you somehow have millions of high-quality labeled examples and ample compute, full fine-tuning may yield incremental gains, but this is rare.
- **How many tasks do you need to support?**
  - If you want separate models for issuer risk classification, ESG controversy extraction, and factor-relevant event tagging, maintaining multiple PEFT heads on a shared base model is far more efficient.

- **What are your latency and memory budgets?**
  - In low-latency settings (e.g., near-real-time news triage), you want to amortize the cost of loading the base model across many tasks. Light-weight adapters are preferable.

A common enterprise pattern is:

1. Standardize on one or two base models that work well on your document mix.
2. Develop a library of task-specific adapters or LoRA modules.
3. Route incoming workload (classification, extraction, summarization) to the base model plus the appropriate adapter configuration.

This mirrors the diagram earlier: the shared transformer stack feeds multiple, domain-adapted heads for different financial tasks.

Preference Optimization for Finance

Many modern models undergo an additional stage beyond pure likelihood training: *preference optimization.* The core idea is to make the model's behavior align with human judgments of quality and safety.

In a financial context, you may care about preferences such as:

- Factual correctness over stylistic flourish.
- Risk-aware language (avoiding unsupported certainty).
- Regulatory safety (no advice that would violate internal or external guidelines).

Technically, this can be implemented with reinforcement learning from human feedback (RLHF) or other alignment techniques, where the model is rewarded for outputs that respect these preferences and penalized for violations.

For your own systems, you likely will not re-run a full RLHF pipeline, but you can apply lighter-weight versions:

- Train or fine-tune small reward models that score outputs for compliance or factuality.
- Use these reward models to filter or rerank candidate outputs from your main model.
- Incorporate automatic checks (e.g., consistency with retrieved data) into your evaluation harness.

This bridges architecture with governance: understanding how to steer a transformer's behavior is as important as knowing how it processes text.

Practical Considerations: Data, Evaluation, and Deployment

Finally, effective domain adaptation is not just about the model; it is about the surrounding process.

Data curation. The value of your adapters or LoRA modules depends entirely on the quality of the examples they see. For each task, you should:

- Define clear labeling guidelines and taxonomies (e.g., specific risk categories).
- Ensure coverage across issuers, sectors, geographies, and regimes.
- Include challenging edge cases (ambiguous language, boilerplate vs. substantive changes).

Evaluation suites. Before deploying an adapted model, evaluate it on:

- **Held-out test sets** that reflect your production data distribution.
- **Stress scenarios**, such as crisis periods, regime shifts, or regulatory changes.

- **Robustness checks**, such as minor wording changes or re-ordered sections.

Latency and cost. Each additional transformer block and each additional adapter adds compute. In practice you may:

- Use smaller models or fewer layers for low-latency triage tasks.
- Reserve larger, more capable models (with richer adapters) for offline research, scenario generation, or high-value decisions.

By combining an understanding of the transformer architecture with disciplined adaptation strategies, you can build models that are not only powerful, but also tractable to operate at scale in real financial environments.

3.2 Embeddings and Vector Indexing

In the previous section we treated the transformer as a powerful engine that ingests sequences of tokens and produces rich internal representations for a wide variety of tasks. In this section, we take a more infrastructural view. Instead of focusing on the internal layers of the model, we focus on *what* we can store and reuse from it: dense vector representations, or *embeddings*.

Embeddings are the numerical language that downstream systems use to reason about financial content. Once we can reliably turn a 10-K, a news article, or an internal research note into a vector, we can build indexes that support fast, semantically meaningful retrieval at scale. That is the backbone of modern retrieval-augmented agents.

From Words to Vectors: Sparse vs. Dense Representations

Before embeddings became common, information retrieval systems largely relied on *sparse* representations.

Sparse representations. A classic bag-of-words or TF–IDF model builds a very high-dimensional vector where each dimension corresponds to a token (word or phrase) in the vocabulary. A document's vector records how often each token appears, possibly weighted by how rare the token is across the corpus.

This has several limitations in finance:

- It is sensitive to exact wording. "Share repurchase" and "stock buyback" are treated as different, unrelated features.
- It is poor at capturing deeper similarity. Two 10-K risk sections that use different language but describe similar exposure (e.g., to European demand) may look dissimilar in sparse space.
- Vectors are very high-dimensional and mostly zeros, which impacts both storage and computational efficiency at scale.

Dense representations (embeddings). In contrast, an embedding model maps a piece of text to a *dense* vector, typically with a few hundred or a few thousand dimensions. Every coordinate is non-zero and meaningful, and similar texts land in similar regions of this vector space.

For example:

- A paragraph describing "weaker-than-expected European demand" and another describing "soft sales in the EU" should be close in embedding space, even if they share few exact words.
- Risk disclosures about supply chain disruptions across different issuers and sectors should cluster together, while still being distinguishable by finer-grained structure.

Dense embeddings exploit the semantic understanding learned by the transformer during pre-training, then optionally refined via domain adaptation. They are crucial for building agents that can search *by meaning* rather than by keyword.

What Exactly Is an Embedding Model Doing?

Conceptually, an embedding model is a transformer whose output has been constrained to be useful for a similarity task. It typically:

1. Tokenizes and embeds the input text (as described in the previous section).
2. Feeds the sequence through several transformer layers.
3. Aggregates the sequence into a single fixed-length vector (for example, by taking the representation of a special "[CLS]" token or by pooling over tokens).

The result is a vector in $\mathbb{R}^d$ (for some dimension d) that summarizes the content. During training, the model is optimized so that texts judged "similar" (e.g., question and relevant answer; two paraphrases of a risk statement) get vectors that are close under a chosen similarity metric.

In practice, you will encounter:

- **Sentence-level models**, optimized to represent short spans like sentences, bullet points, or brief news headlines.
- **Document-level models**, better suited for longer inputs like complete 10-K sections or multi-paragraph research notes.

For financial agents, you often work somewhere in between: chunked sections of longer documents that are large enough to carry context, but small enough to be indexed and retrieved efficiently.

Handling Financial Structure: Tables, Code-Like Text, and Hybrids

Financial documents are not homogeneous prose. They contain:

- Narrative sections (MD&A, risk factors).
- Tables of numbers (income statements, segment breakdowns).

- Code-like artifacts (XBRL tags, formulaic disclosures).
- Bullet lists, footnotes, and boilerplate.

A straightforward text embedding model can generally handle mixed text and numbers, but certain structures deserve special care:

- **Tables.** You may choose to linearize tables (row by row, with headers inserted as labels) before embedding. For example, "Revenue, North America, $3.2bn, up 5%" becomes a text sequence. For heavy quantitative use, embeddings are often paired with structured features rather than used alone.
- **Tagged or templated text.** XBRL tags, tickers, and standardized codes (e.g., SIC, NAICS) should be preserved because they are semantically rich. A well-trained embedding model can learn that certain tags correlate with specific financial concepts.

The guiding principle is consistency: whatever preprocessing pipeline you use, apply it in the same way to both your documents and your queries, so they live in the same embedding space.

Similarity Metrics: Measuring Distance in Embedding Space

Once you have embeddings for documents and queries, you need a way to measure how similar they are. Common choices include:

- **Cosine similarity.** Measures the angle between two vectors. It is unaffected by the magnitude (length) of the vectors and focuses on direction. This is widely used because it captures "semantic alignment" independent of scale.
- **Inner product (dot product).** Multiplies corresponding coordinates and sums. Closely related to cosine similarity if vectors are normalized. Some embedding models are trained explicitly to maximize inner product between related items.

- **Euclidean distance.** Measures straight-line distance between two points in vector space. Less common as a direct metric for text embeddings, but under certain training setups it is equivalent to or compatible with the above.

In practice, your choice is driven by the embedding model and the index implementation:

- Many off-the-shelf models assume cosine similarity or inner product.
- Vector databases and ANN (approximate nearest neighbor) libraries often support all three, but may be optimized for one.

The key is to match the metric used in your index to the one implicit in the model's training. Misalignment here can degrade retrieval quality even if embeddings themselves are strong.

From Embeddings to Indexes: Why We Need Specialized Structures

If you only had a few thousand documents, you could compute similarity between a query embedding and every document embedding on the fly: a straightforward matrix-vector multiplication.

In real financial environments, you face:

- Millions of documents (historical filings, broker notes, research archives).
- Continuous inflows of news, social media, and internal commentary.
- Latency targets ranging from tens of milliseconds (for live trading or alerting) to seconds (for research workflows).

Brute-force search scales linearly with the number of vectors and is quickly too slow. Instead, we build *vector indexes*: data structures that organize embeddings so we can retrieve the nearest neighbors efficiently.

Dense vs. Sparse, Revisited: Hybrid Search

Before diving into index variants, it is worth noting that many production systems combine:

- **Semantic similarity** via dense embeddings, and
- **Symbolic filters and sparse signals** such as ticker, date, language, and exact keyword matches.

For example, you might first filter to all documents with ticker "AAPL" in the past three years, then run semantic similarity on that subset. Or you might boost scores for documents where the query terms appear as exact phrases.

This *hybrid search* approach allows you to honor hard constraints (e.g., only issuers under current coverage) while still benefiting from the semantic generalization of embeddings.

The Embedding Pipeline in Practice

We can now outline the typical pipeline that turns raw financial documents into an indexed embedding store, and later uses it to answer semantic queries.

After we introduce the basic pipeline in words, the following diagram anchors the concepts visually.

1. **Ingest documents.** Collect 10-Ks, earnings-call transcripts, news, research notes, and internal commentary. Apply basic cleaning (encoding fixes, markup removal).
2. **Chunk and normalize.** Split long documents into manageable chunks (for example, 300–800 tokens) that preserve logical structure: paragraphs, sections, or table rows.
3. **Embed each chunk.** Run an embedding model to produce a dense vector for each chunk. Store accompanying metadata (ticker, date, source, section type).

4. **Build an index.** Insert all vectors into a vector index that supports fast nearest-neighbor search under your chosen similarity metric.

5. **Query.** When a user or agent issues a query (natural-language question, factor description, or example snippet), embed the query, search the index, and retrieve the most similar chunks.

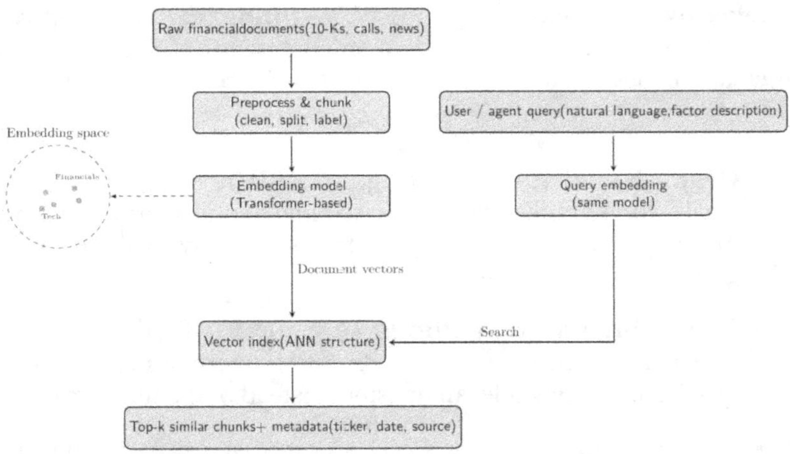

This pipeline is the foundation on which more sophisticated retrieval-augmented generation and agentic systems are built.

Index Variants: Flat vs. Approximate Nearest Neighbor

At the core of a vector index is the nearest-neighbor problem: given a query vector, find the k most similar document vectors according to your metric. There are two broad categories of indexes:

Flat indexes (exact search). The simplest structure stores all embeddings in a contiguous array. A query search computes similarity to every vector and selects the top k.

- **Pros:** Exact results; conceptually simple; easy to implement and debug.
- **Cons:** Time and cost scale linearly with the number of vectors. For millions of documents, this can become too slow for low-latency use.

Flat indexes are perfectly acceptable for small corpora or offline research tools where latency is less critical.

Approximate nearest neighbor (ANN) indexes. For larger corpora, approximate methods trade a small amount of accuracy for a large gain in speed and memory efficiency. Several families are popular:

- **Graph-based methods (e.g., HNSW).** Build a navigable small-world graph of vectors where edges connect nearby points. At query time, the algorithm performs a greedy search over the graph to find neighbors.
- **Clustering-based methods (e.g., IVF).** Partition vectors into clusters (inverted file lists). At query time, search is restricted to a few relevant clusters instead of the full dataset.
- **Product quantization (PQ).** Compress vectors by approximating them with combinations of smaller codebooks, significantly reducing memory footprint and enabling faster distance computations.

Modern vector databases often combine several ideas (e.g., HNSW over PQ-compressed vectors) and handle many low-level details for you. The main design question becomes: what balance of recall, latency, and memory suits your workload?

Designing for Financial Workloads

Financial research and trading workloads place distinct demands on vector indexes. A few common scenarios illustrate the trade-offs.

Live agents and alerting. Suppose you run an intraday agent that:

- Monitors a real-time news feed,
- Embeds incoming headlines and short stories,
- For each new story, retrieves similar historical events and related issuer disclosures.

Here, you care about:

- Low latency (tens of milliseconds).
- Fast updates (new items must be searchable quickly).
- Good, but not necessarily perfect, recall.

Graph-based ANN structures like HNSW, tuned for quick insertions and queries, are often appropriate. You might operate separate indexes per asset class or region to bound search space further.

Offline research and strategy development. In a research setting, an analyst might:

- Formulate a factor narrative (e.g., "exposure to European consumer demand"),
- Retrieve a large set of semantically similar disclosures across sectors and years,
- Use them as inputs to a backtesting pipeline.

Here, you can tolerate higher latency and heavier computation in exchange for deeper recall and richer filtering options. You might:

- Use higher recall settings in your ANN index.
- Combine vector search with SQL filters on metadata.
- Run multi-pass retrieval: coarse semantic search, then fine re-ranking with a larger model.

Regulatory and compliance queries. Compliance teams may need to:

- Search historical communications (emails, chat, research) for patterns of language,
- Respond to regulator inquiries that require thorough coverage.

Here, *coverage* and *auditability* matter more than speed. You might use:

- Exact search or very high-recall ANN settings.
- Logging and versioning of indexes (e.g., snapshots by date).
- Strict integration with access controls and data governance systems.

The underlying mechanisms (embeddings and vector indexes) are the same, but the configuration changes with the application.

Time-Aware and Ticker-Aware Indexing

Financial information is intrinsically temporal and issuer-specific. Two simple but powerful design patterns are:

Time-aware indexes. Instead of a single monolithic index, you can:

- Partition by time (e.g., yearly or quarterly indexes).
- Encode date ranges in metadata and filter at query time.

This allows questions like:

> "Retrieve similar risk disclosures, but only from the three years preceding this event."

It also supports backtesting: you can constrain retrieval to information that would have been available at a given historical date, avoiding look-ahead bias.

Ticker-aware indexes. For issuer-centric analysis, you often want to retrieve:

- All embeddings related to a specific ticker,
- Or neighborhoods of related issuers (peers, supply chain links).

You can store ticker and sector in metadata and apply filters before or after vector search. Later, when we introduce knowledge graphs, we will see how embedding-based retrieval can be combined with graph traversal to answer questions like "Which suppliers share this risk pattern?"

Index Hygiene: Updates, Deletions, and Drift

Vector indexes, like any data structure in production, need maintenance.

Updates and deletions. Corporate actions, restatements, and reclassifications mean:

- New documents must be embedded and inserted continuously.
- Old or superseded documents may need to be marked as inactive or removed.

Some ANN structures support incremental updates well; others may require periodic rebuilds to maintain efficiency. For regulatory reasons, you should track which index version was used to answer which query.

Monitoring embedding quality. Over time, your embedding model or your document mix may change. This can cause *embedding drift*: the same type of text is mapped to a different region of space than before, potentially degrading retrieval.

Practical steps include:

- Maintaining a benchmark set of query-document pairs with known relevance, and tracking retrieval quality over time.
- Visualizing cluster structure for key concepts (e.g., risk categories) to ensure they remain well-separated.
- Re-embedding and re-indexing the corpus when you upgrade or significantly retrain your embedding model.

Putting It All Together for Agentic Systems

Embeddings and vector indexes are not an end in themselves; they are the substrate on which agentic research and trading systems operate.

When a generative agent answers "Why did this stock move today?" or "Show me disclosures similar to this guidance change," it is usually:

1. Embedding the question.
2. Retrieving semantically similar chunks from one or more vector indexes, often with ticker/time filters.
3. Feeding those retrieved passages back into a transformer model as context for generation.

In the next sections, we will connect these pieces into full retrieval-augmented generation (RAG) architectures and issuer-centric knowledge systems. The conceptual groundwork laid here—mapping text to vectors, and organizing those vectors for fast similarity search—is what allows those higher-level systems to be both powerful and practical in real financial environments.

3.3 Prompt Engineering and Long-Context Techniques

In the previous sections we treated the transformer and its embeddings as infrastructure: they tell us *what* the model can represent and *how* we can retrieve relevant information. In this section we shift perspective from infrastructure to *interaction design*. Given a powerful base model and access to retrieval and tools, how do we reliably get the behavior we want for real research and trading workflows, without wasting compute or inviting unwanted surprises?

Prompt engineering and long-context techniques are best understood as a form of lightweight programming. Instead of writing code in Python or C++, we are programming the system with carefully structured natural language, examples, and tool specifications. The same discipline applies: we care about correctness, robustness, and cost.

Thinking of Prompts as Contracts

A useful mental model is to think of a prompt as a *contract* between you and the model:

- You specify the *role* the model should play (for example, a credit analyst, a risk officer, or a research assistant).
- You describe the *task* and any constraints (for example, "do not give investment advice", "never fabricate numbers", "output a JSON object with these fields").
- The model agrees, as best it can, to behave within that contract.

Vague or underspecified contracts produce vague or unpredictable behavior. Carefully written prompts, with clear roles and explicit constraints, tend to produce far more stable outputs and are easier to integrate into automated systems.

In a finance setting, that contract often needs to encode:

- Regulatory awareness (no personal advice, no material non-public information, disciplined language around uncertainty).
- Output formats tailored to downstream systems (CSV-like tables, JSON for risk engines, bullet lists for analysts).
- Domain framing (are we doing exploratory analysis, formal reporting, or compliance checks?).

Instruction Templates and Role Specification

Instead of writing bespoke prompts for each query, it is better to define *instruction templates* that can be reused across tasks. A typical template might include:

1. **Role.** "You are a buy-side equity analyst specializing in U.S. large-cap technology stocks."
2. **Objective.** "Your job is to read financial disclosures and extract structured information relevant to valuation and risk."

3. **Constraints.** "Do not offer investment recommendations. When you are uncertain, say that explicitly and explain why."
4. **Input description.** "You will receive an excerpt from a 10-K filing and associated metadata (ticker, date, section)."
5. **Output schema.** "Return a JSON object with fields `risk_factors`, `growth_drivers`, and `accounting_notes`. Each should be a list of short bullet points."

Once this template is defined, your orchestration layer can fill in the input section dynamically with specific documents or retrieved passages. The model sees a stable structure each time, which helps with robustness and testability.

Role specification is especially important when the same underlying model is used for different workflows:

- A "compliance officer" role might be risk-averse and conservative in interpretation.
- A "research assistant" role might prioritize coverage and hypothesis generation.
- A "data normalizer" role might focus purely on structured extraction with no narrative commentary.

Although the model's internal weights are the same, the role description steers how it interprets ambiguities and trade-offs.

Structured Prompting Patterns

Beyond simple instructions, there are recurring patterns that help the model reason more reliably. These patterns are particularly helpful for complex financial tasks, such as multi-step event analysis or scenario construction.

Decomposition Prompts

Complex questions often benefit from being broken into simpler subquestions. For example, consider:

> "How has Company X's exposure to European consumer demand evolved over the last five years, and what are the main risks implied for its current valuation?"

A decomposition prompt might instruct the model to:

1. Identify and summarize all relevant disclosures about European demand for each year.
2. Compare and describe the changes across years.
3. Enumerate the implied risk channels (volume, pricing, FX, regulatory).
4. Synthesize a final view relating those trends to valuation drivers.

You can implement this either as:

- A single prompt that tells the model to think in steps and label each step clearly, or
- A multi-call workflow where your agent orchestrates separate model calls for each sub-step and passes intermediate summaries forward.

The latter is more work to implement but often easier to monitor and debug.

Chain-of-Thought and Self-Explanation

Chain-of-thought prompting encourages the model to show its reasoning rather than jumping directly to a conclusion. For numerical or logical tasks (e.g., reconciling numbers across filings, checking consistency of guidance), this can increase reliability.

For instance, instead of asking:

> "Is the company's guidance consistent with its historical margin trends? Yes or no."

you might ask:

> "Compare the company's current guidance with its historical margin trends. First, summarize the last three years of margin data. Next, restate the current guidance numerically. Then, explain step by step whether the guidance appears conservative, aggressive, or in line with history. Finally, give a one-sentence conclusion."

However, chain-of-thought has costs:

- It generates more tokens, increasing latency and compute.
- It may not add much value for simple classification or extraction tasks.

A good rule of thumb is to reserve explicit chain-of-thought for tasks where you truly need the intermediate reasoning (for example, compliance audit trails or complex reconciliations), and keep prompts lean for high-volume or latency-sensitive tasks.

Self-Checking and Critic Patterns

To reduce hallucinations and improve factuality, you can prompt the model to act as its own critic. A simple pattern is:

1. First, answer the question normally.
2. Then, in a separate step or separate model call, ask the model to review its own answer for:
    - Unsupported claims,
    - Numerical inconsistencies,
    - Violations of specified constraints (e.g., offering advice).

For example:

> "You previously produced the following summary of Company Y's liquidity position. Review that summary. Highlight any statements that are not directly supported by the cited text excerpts. Suggest corrections or mark them as uncertain."

This pattern can be particularly effective when combined with retrieval: the critic is explicitly asked to cross-check the answer against the retrieved passages or structured data.

Tool Invocation: Making the Model Call External Systems

In realistic financial agents, the model does not operate in isolation. It often needs to:

- Look up prices or time series from a market data API.
- Query an internal risk engine for VaR or exposure.
- Pull additional documents from a search index or knowledge graph.

Modern LLM frameworks support *tool calls*: the model is given a catalog of tools, each with a name and a structured schema for its arguments, and it decides when and how to call them.

Prompt design plays a central role here:

- You describe each tool in natural language, focusing on what it does and when it should be used.
- You instruct the model to prefer tools over guessing, especially for numerical or factual queries.
- You specify how to handle failures (e.g., missing data, API errors).

A well-written tool description might be:

> **Name:** get_ohlcv.
> **Purpose:** Retrieve historical open-high-low-close-volume data for a given ticker and date range. Use this tool whenever you need actual market prices rather than approximations. If the tool returns no data, explain that the data is unavailable instead of guessing.

The orchestration layer is then responsible for:

1. Detecting tool calls in the model's output,
2. Executing the corresponding external function,
3. Providing the results back to the model in a structured format for further reasoning.

In this setup, prompt engineering is about making tool usage predictable and constrained. You want the model to call tools when appropriate, not at random; and you want it to handle tool outputs reliably.

Validating and Post-Processing Tool Outputs

Even with good tooling prompts, you should not treat the model's interpretation of tool outputs as ground truth. Practical safeguards include:

- **Schema validation.** Require that outputs follow strict schemas (for example, JSON with specific fields and types). Reject or repair outputs that do not validate.
- **Range checks.** For numerical fields (returns, spreads, volumes), apply sanity checks. If a model reports a 10,000% daily return, flag it.
- **Cross-source checks.** Where possible, corroborate key facts with multiple tools or data sources.

You can encode some of these constraints in prompts ("if any value is outside this range, mark it as suspect"), but many are better enforced at the orchestration layer. Think of the model as a flexible reasoner, not as an infallible gatekeeper.

Long-Context Techniques: Coping with Financial Document Scale

Financial texts are long. A multi-year sequence of earnings-call transcripts, or a complete 10-K with exhibits, can easily exceed the context window of even large models. Naively stuffing everything into the prompt is expensive and often ineffective.

Several complementary techniques help manage long context.

Sliding-Window Prompts

The simplest approach is to process a long document in overlapping chunks. For example:

- Split the text into windows of 2,000 tokens with 200-token overlaps.
- Run the model separately on each window to extract events, risks, or themes.
- Merge or reconcile the results across windows.

Sliding windows are straightforward to implement and parallelize. However, they have limitations:

- The model's view is local; global patterns that span many windows may be missed.
- There is duplication across windows, increasing total token usage.

Sliding windows work well when local context is sufficient (e.g., classifying paragraphs) but are less suitable for tasks that require holistic understanding of a document.

Hierarchical Summarization

For truly long documents or multi-document collections, a hierarchical approach is more appropriate:

1. At the lowest level, summarize or extract key points from small chunks (sections, paragraphs).
2. At the next level, combine these into higher-level summaries (per document, per period).
3. At the top level, integrate across documents (e.g., multi-year trends, cross-issuer comparisons).

Each level uses the model with a manageable context size, and intermediate summaries become a kind of *compressed memory*. For example:

- Level 1: Summaries of each quarter's earnings-call Q&A for a company.
- Level 2: A yearly narrative summarizing that year's calls.
- Level 3: A five-year strategic evolution summary.

You can then answer queries using the compressed representations, calling back to the original text only when necessary. This dramatically reduces token usage while preserving the big picture.

Retrieval-Augmented Context Building

The embedding and vector indexing machinery from the previous section provides another key tool: instead of trying to feed the model *all* relevant text, we can retrieve the *most relevant* passages for each query.

A retrieval-augmented prompt looks something like:

1. The system instructs: "You will be given a user question and several excerpts from financial documents that are relevant to that question. Base your answer only on these excerpts. If the excerpts do not contain enough information, state that explicitly."
2. The agent embeds the user's query and retrieves the top k relevant chunks from the index.
3. Those chunks are placed in the prompt, along with the question and any constraints.

This approach (which we will formalize as RAG in the next section) is central to long-context management:

- It limits context size by selecting only the most promising passages.
- It makes provenance explicit: the answer is grounded in specific retrieved texts.

- It reduces hallucinations, since the model is asked to stick to the provided evidence.

Prompt design plays a crucial role: you must be explicit that the model should not invent facts beyond the retrieved context, and you should ask it to cite which excerpt supports which claim.

Memory Patterns for Ongoing Workflows

Many research and trading workflows are not one-off questions, but ongoing sessions:

- An analyst iteratively refines a thesis over dozens of turns.
- A risk manager runs a daily check on similar metrics but with new data.
- A trading agent reacts to a series of intraday events.

Naively appending all past turns into a single ever-growing prompt is costly and eventually exceeds context limits. Instead, we need simple *memory patterns*.

Summarized conversation memory. Periodically replace the full interaction history with a compressed summary that preserves key decisions, hypotheses, and constraints. For example, after every 10 turns:

- Ask the model (or a smaller summarization model) to produce a structured summary of the session so far.
- Store that summary in a separate memory store.
- For subsequent turns, include only the latest few exchanges plus the summary.

External state vs. conversational memory. Distinguish between:

- *Ephemeral conversational context* (how we got here), and

- *Persistent state* (current set of tickers under analysis, chosen factor definitions, risk thresholds).

Persistent state often belongs in explicit data structures managed by your system (for example, a configuration object or small database), not in the free-form prompt. The prompt can refer to this state succinctly ("use the current coverage universe from the portfolio object"), while the orchestration layer injects the relevant structured data as needed.

Cost and Latency Control

All of these techniques have one overarching constraint in production: you have finite budget for tokens, compute, and latency. Practical recipes for keeping costs under control include:

- **Router prompts.** Use a small, cheap model to decide whether a query needs a large model at all, or whether it can be answered by a template, a simple rule, or a cache.

- **Adaptive context sizing.** Adjust the number of retrieved passages or the depth of chain-of-thought based on query complexity. A simple classification request does not need a 10-step reasoning trace.

- **Intermediate compression.** When chaining multiple model calls, avoid passing full outputs forward if a compressed representation will do (for example, using bullet-point summaries instead of full text).

- **Batching and parallelism.** For offline jobs (e.g., scoring risk disclosures across a universe), batch multiple prompts in a single model call where supported, and run independent tasks in parallel.

Prompt engineering is therefore not just about getting the *right* behavior, but the *right behavior at the right price.*

Evaluating Prompt Designs Before Production

Finally, because prompts are effectively programs, you should test them with the same seriousness you apply to quantitative strategies. A minimal prompt evaluation loop includes:

- **A fixed test suite** of representative queries, documents, and expected behaviors (including edge cases and stress scenarios).
- **Automatic checks** for format correctness, constraint violations, and obvious hallucinations.
- **Version control** for prompts and configurations, so you can compare old vs. new behaviors and roll back if needed.

Small changes in wording can have nontrivial effects. Systematically testing prompts before they hit production reduces surprises and gives you confidence that your agentic systems will behave as designed when exposed to live financial data.

With a solid understanding of prompt engineering and long-context techniques, we are now ready to connect all the pieces: transformers, embeddings, retrieval, and prompts, into full retrieval-augmented generation systems and knowledge graphs tailored to financial research and trading.

3.4 Retrieval-Augmented Generation and Knowledge Graphs

In the previous sections we treated generative models as powerful but data-hungry engines. We saw how transformers internally represent text, how embeddings allow us to search large financial corpora by meaning, and how careful prompt design and long-context techniques keep these models usable in real workflows. We now put these pieces together into systems that are not only fluent, but also *grounded* in verifiable financial data.

This section has two main goals:

- Explain retrieval-augmented generation (RAG) in financial terms, and show how to build robust retrieval pipelines on top of your embedding and indexing infrastructure.
- Introduce issuer-centric knowledge graphs and show how to combine graph structure with unstructured retrieval so that answers are linked back to entities, events, and auditable evidence.

The unifying theme is control: we want our agents to say, in effect, "Here is my answer, and here is exactly where I got it."

What Is Retrieval-Augmented Generation in Finance?

A bare language model answers questions based on its pre-training. It has no built-in notion of the latest 10-Q, yesterday's earnings call, or a proprietary broker note that only your firm has. It will often try to "fill in the gaps" from patterns it has seen elsewhere, which leads to hallucinations.

Retrieval-augmented generation (RAG) addresses this by putting a retrieval step in front of the model:

1. Given a question or task, the system first retrieves relevant documents or passages from an external knowledge store (vector indexes, databases, knowledge graphs).
2. The model then generates an answer *conditioned explicitly* on those retrieved pieces of evidence.

In a financial setting, this means:

- The agent does not improvise an income statement; it retrieves the reported numbers.
- It does not invent a merger rumor; it cites specific news or filings.
- It can operate on proprietary content (internal research, house views) that was never part of its original training data.

The retrieval step turns a general-purpose generative model into an interface for your firm's actual information.

An End-to-End View of RAG with Knowledge Graphs

Before we dive into individual components, it is helpful to have a high-level picture of how everything fits together: documents, embeddings, vector indexes, knowledge graphs, and the generative model.

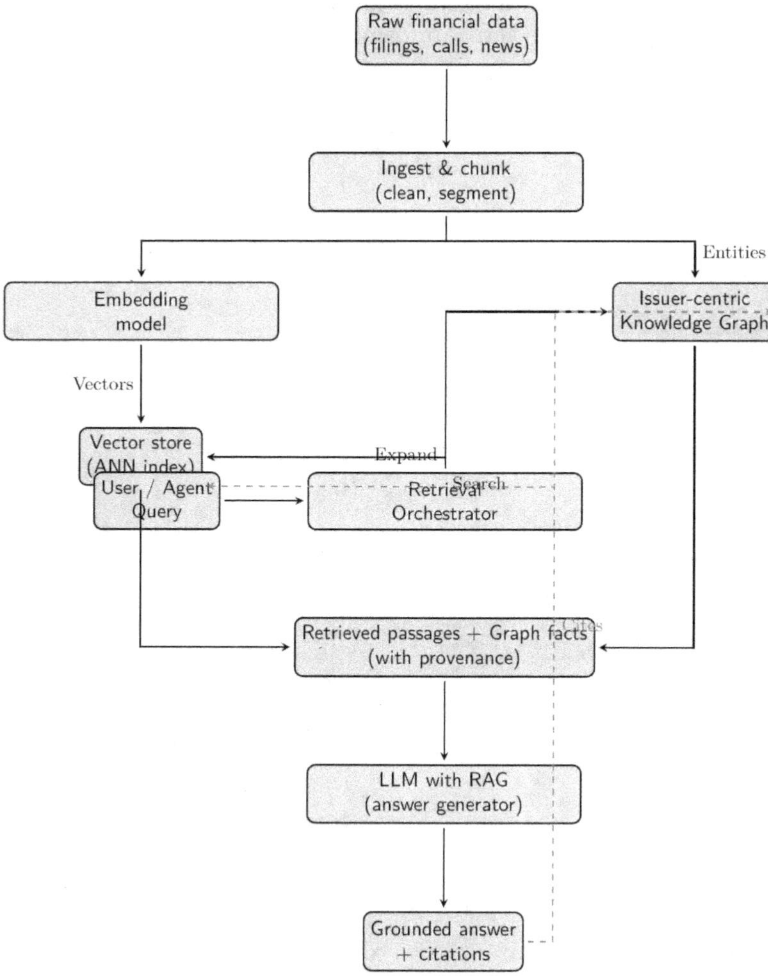

The bottom tier shows how your firm's raw data is processed into two complementary stores:

- A **vector store** for semantic retrieval over unstructured chunks of text.
- A **knowledge graph** encoding entities (issuers, instruments,

people), events, and relationships (ownership, supply chains, corporate actions).

The top tier shows how a user query is embedded, used to retrieve text and graph facts, and finally passed to the LLM, which generates a grounded answer with explicit provenance.

Building the Retrieval Pipeline

The retrieval pipeline is the bridge between the user's question and the relevant parts of your knowledge base. It builds directly on the embedding and indexing concepts from the previous section.

A typical retrieval pipeline for financial text comprises the following steps:

1. Query understanding and embedding. The system receives a query:

> "Why did Ticker ABC fall 7% on March 3, 2024?"

It constructs a representation that includes:

- The raw natural-language question.
- Extracted entities (ticker ABC, date 2024-03-03).
- An embedding of the question for semantic similarity search.

2. Document retrieval via vector search. Using the query embedding and metadata filters (ticker, date window, region), the system queries the vector index. It might search across:

- News headlines and stories.
- Earnings-call transcripts.
- Internal notes tagged to that ticker.

The result is a ranked list of chunks, each with text and metadata such as source, timestamp, and section type.

3. Evidence selection and trimming. To fit within the model's context window and cost budget, we cannot pass everything to the LLM. We therefore:

- Select the top k chunks (for example, 10–20), perhaps with diversification across sources and time.
- Trim or compress overly long chunks (for example, summarizing a full article down to the relevant paragraph).

4. Packaging evidence into a prompt. The selected evidence is arranged into a structured prompt segment, often with explicit labels:

> **Document 1 (News, 2024-03-03 10:15 UTC)**: *[text]*
> **Document 2 (Earnings call, 2024-03-02)**: *[text]*
> ...

The system prompt then instructs the model to answer based *only* on this evidence, and to reference document IDs when making claims.

Common Pitfalls in Financial RAG

Several failure modes are common when applying RAG to financial data:

Over-chunking. If documents are split into extremely small fragments (for example, individual sentences), each chunk may lose the surrounding context needed to interpret it correctly. A single sentence about "weaker demand" is ambiguous without knowing which region or product line it refers to.

In practice, chunks should align with natural financial structure: full risk-factor paragraphs, answer blocks in Q&A, or table rows with their headers.

Ignoring temporal constraints. Financial queries are almost always time-sensitive. Without explicit date filters, retrieval may surface outdated information:

- A risk disclosure from five years ago that was later resolved.
- Pre- and post-event commentary mixed together, introducing look-ahead bias in backtests.

For any query with a reference date (e.g., "as of March 2022"), your retrieval layer should enforce that only information available up to that date is considered, with explicit handling of restatements and corrections.

Weak provenance. If answers are not tied back to specific documents and locations (file name, page, timestamp), they become hard to audit. This is especially problematic for:

- Compliance and regulatory responses.
- Investment committee memos that rely on agent-generated analysis.

Your RAG prompts should require the model to cite which document supports each key claim, and your UI or downstream systems should make it easy to navigate from the answer back to those sources.

Issuer-Centric Knowledge Graphs

Vector search over text is powerful, but it does not explicitly encode relationships like:

- "Company A owns 80% of Subsidiary B."
- "Supplier S provides 40% of component X to Issuer I."
- "Fund F holds Bond B and Equity E of Issuer I."

To capture such structured relationships, we use a *knowledge graph*. At a high level, a knowledge graph is:

- A set of **nodes** representing entities and concepts: issuers, instruments, people, events, sectors, geographies.

- A set of **edges** representing typed relationships between nodes: "owns", "supplies", "is subsidiary of", "announces", "is in sector".

For financial use, a typical graph might include:

- **Issuer nodes** with attributes such as ticker, legal name, country, sector, and key fundamentals.
- **Instrument nodes** (equities, bonds, derivatives) linked to their issuers.
- **Event nodes** for earnings releases, guidance updates, M&A announcements, rating changes, and macro events.
- **Ownership and exposure edges**, such as cross-holdings, supply-chain dependencies, and index membership.

This structure is especially valuable for questions that cross issuers, instruments, or asset classes, for example:

> "Which of our portfolio holdings are indirectly exposed to this semiconductor supplier's factory closure?"
> "List all issuers whose main customers are in the energy sector and that have negative guidance revisions in the last quarter."

A pure text-based RAG pipeline would struggle to answer these reliably. A knowledge graph, when combined with text retrieval, makes them much more tractable.

Connecting Text to the Graph: Entity Linking

To integrate unstructured documents with a knowledge graph, we must *link* text spans to graph entities. A typical pipeline involves:

1. **Named entity recognition (NER).** Detect mentions of companies, people, instruments, and locations in the text.
2. **Disambiguation.** Map each mention to the correct graph node:

- "Apple" → AAPL (the company) vs. the fruit.
- "GM" → General Motors vs. "gross margin."

3. **Edge creation.** For example, when a news article mentions that "Company X acquired Company Y," you might create an "acquired" edge from X to Y, and an "announced-in" edge from the event node to the article.

Embedding models can assist in disambiguation, but often you will supplement them with rule-based logic (tickers, regulator IDs, ISINs) and reference databases.

Once entity linking is in place, your retrieval pipeline can:

- Filter or boost documents mentioning specific entities or their graph neighbors.
- Enrich retrieved passages with structured facts about the entities involved.

Marrying Retrieval and Graph Traversal

The most powerful systems treat the vector store and the knowledge graph as complementary, not competing, sources.

A typical hybrid workflow might look like this:

Example: "Why did this stock move today?"

Given a query about Ticker ABC's price move:

1. **Graph lookup.** Use the graph to find:
   - The issuer node for ABC.
   - Recent event nodes linked to that issuer (earnings releases, guidance changes, major news).
   - Related entities: key suppliers, major customers, sector peers.
2. **Text retrieval.** For each promising event or related entity:

   - Retrieve specific news articles, filings, or internal notes via the vector store.

3. **Evidence assembly.** Construct a bundle of:

   - Event facts from the graph (e.g., "Earnings surprise: +5%; Guidance revised down for European segment").
   - Supporting passages from text sources.

4. **Generation.** Prompt the LLM to synthesize an explanation, clearly tying its reasoning to both structured facts and retrieved text, and explicitly labeling uncertainty if multiple plausible drivers exist.

Conversely, you can start from text and move into the graph:

Example: "Show cross-issuer risk views for this topic."

Suppose an analyst wants to understand "exposure to European consumer demand" across a portfolio:

1. **Text-driven retrieval.** Use an embedding of that phrase to retrieve risk disclosures and guidance passages from many issuers.

2. **Entity extraction.** For each passage, extract the issuers, products, and geographies mentioned, and link them to graph nodes.

3. **Graph aggregation.** Traverse the graph to:

   - Group exposures by sector and region.
   - Identify shared suppliers or customers.

4. **Generation.** Ask the LLM to summarize the cross-issuer picture, again citing both the specific disclosures and the aggregated graph view.

In both directions, retrieval and graph traversal can reinforce each other: text provides nuance and unstructured detail; graphs provide structure and connectivity.

Designing Prompts for Groundedness and Provenance

To get the most out of RAG with knowledge graphs, your prompts must emphasize groundedness. A good system prompt might say:

- "Base your answer only on the evidence passages and structured facts provided."
- "If the evidence is insufficient to answer confidently, say so and explain what is missing."
- "Cite the document ID and graph entity (e.g., ticker, event ID) for each key claim."

You can further encourage traceability by enforcing an output structure, for example:

- A section listing *evidence items* with their sources.
- A section listing *inferences* drawn from that evidence, each tagged with supporting items.
- A section highlighting *assumptions or uncertainties.*

This discipline turns the model's output into something closer to an analyst memo: a chain of reasoning anchored in explicit sources, not a free-form essay.

Evaluation and Governance

Because RAG systems operate at the intersection of unstructured text, structured data, and model behavior, their evaluation must go beyond traditional accuracy metrics.

Key dimensions include:

Groundedness. Do the model's claims match the retrieved evidence and graph facts?

- You can measure this with human labeling on a test set, or with secondary models trained to detect unsupported claims.

Coverage. Does retrieval surface the *right* documents and entities?

- Evaluate recall by checking how often known-relevant documents appear in the top k results.
- For graph queries, verify that the traversal logic finds all relevant neighbors for a set of benchmark cases.

Provenance quality. Are citations and entity references correct and useful?

- Spot-check that cited page numbers, sections, and event IDs actually contain the claimed information.
- Ensure that any downstream user (analyst, risk manager, regulator) can trace the answer back without ambiguity.

Robustness and bias. Does the system behave sensibly during stressed markets, regime changes, or when information is sparse?

- Include crisis periods and edge cases in your test suite.
- Watch for systematic under- or over-weighting of particular sources or entity types.

Governance-wise, treat your RAG system like any other critical model:

- Version-control your retrieval configurations, graphs, and prompts.
- Log queries, retrieved evidence, and final answers for audit.
- Define clear responsibilities for reviewing and updating data pipelines and graph schemas.

Bringing It All Together

Retrieval-augmented generation and knowledge graphs transform large language models from generic text generators into *interfaces* for your firm's financial knowledge. By:

- Using embeddings and vector indexes to find relevant unstructured content,
- Encoding entities and relationships in an issuer-centric graph,
- Linking documents to graph nodes via entity recognition and disambiguation,
- And carefully designing prompts that demand grounded, cited answers,

you can build agents that answer complex, cross-cutting financial questions while remaining anchored in verifiable, entity-linked data.

These systems are not a replacement for human analysts or risk managers. Rather, they extend their reach: surfacing connections across massive document corpora and intricate ownership networks, while providing the traceability, control, and auditability that modern financial institutions require.

Chapter 4

Agentic Systems and Orchestration

Trading desks and research teams do not need another smart chatbot; they need systems that wake up with the market, watch signals, call models and data, and act-while staying inside strict risk, cost, and compliance rails. This chapter shows how to turn raw LLM capabilities into disciplined financial agents: entities that perceive the world through tools and data, maintain state and memory, plan across multiple steps (and multiple agents), and remain auditable enough that a risk manager would sign off on them.

4.1 Agent Design Patterns and Control Loops

In earlier chapters we treated large language models (LLMs) mostly as powerful but passive components: you send in a prompt, you receive a completion, and you interpret or post-process the result. Financial work, however, is rarely a single-shot exercise. Traders, analysts, and risk managers operate in loops: they observe markets and portfolios, think through implications and constraints, and then take actions that in turn change what they will observe next. In this section we introduce *agentic* systems—LLM-based programs that are explicitly designed around this perception–reasoning–action cycle—and show how to wrap a model in a robust control structure suitable for real financial workflows.

From One-Off Completions to Agents

A one-off completion is a single interaction:

1. You prompt the model with some context (e.g., a news headline and a ticker).
2. The model responds once (e.g., a qualitative summary or a suggested trade idea).

This is useful for ad hoc analysis, but it falls short when:

- You must integrate live data feeds (prices, news, risk metrics).
- You need multi-step reasoning (fetch, analyze, cross-check, then decide).
- You must respect strict constraints (risk limits, compliance policies, latency).
- You need repeatable, auditable behavior over long horizons.

An **agent** is an LLM embedded in a control loop that repeatedly:

- **Perceives** the state of the world and its own context (market data, portfolio, prior steps).
- **Reasons** about objectives, constraints, and uncertainties (what should happen next, given what I know?).
- **Acts** by calling tools or emitting decisions that can change the state (query data, compute analytics, stage orders, write reports).

This cycle can repeat many times in a single task (e.g., building a trade basket) or indefinitely in a live service (e.g., an intraday news triage agent).

Right after this conceptual definition, it is helpful to have a concrete picture of the components involved and how they connect.

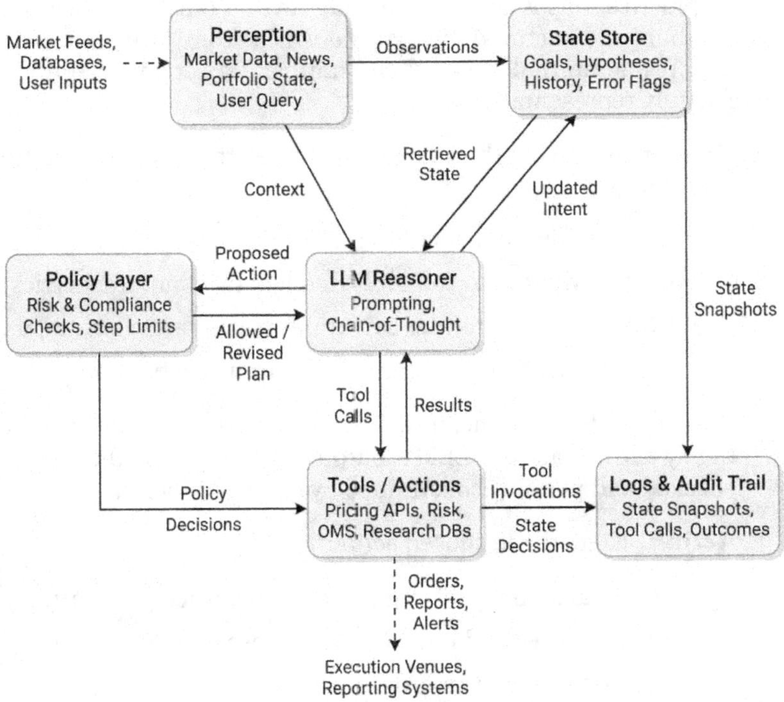

The Perception–Reasoning–Action Loop in Finance

The core loop can be written conceptually as:

1. **Perception.** Gather all relevant inputs for the current step:

   - Market data: prices, volumes, spreads, implied vols.
   - Event data: news, earnings releases, macro prints.
   - Portfolio state: positions, P&L, risk metrics, limits.
   - Task state: what the agent has already done and what remains.
   - User instructions: a new request, override, or clarification.

   In practice, this is not just "reading text." Perception means assembling a structured view of the world from APIs, databases, and prior internal state, then summarizing it into a prompt-friendly representation.

2. **Reasoning.** Use the LLM to interpret the current situation given the goal:

   - Identify what information is missing.
   - Decide whether to call tools (fetch data, compute metrics).
   - Evaluate options under constraints (e.g., risk, cost, latency).
   - Plan the next step or, if finished, produce a final output.

   Reasoning does *not* mean the model is trusted blindly. Instead, the system treats the LLM's output as a proposal that will be checked and possibly constrained by explicit policies.

3. **Action.** Execute the chosen action:

   - Call an analytics tool (e.g., risk engine, pricing library).
   - Retrieve external knowledge (e.g., research notes, filings).
   - Stage or simulate an order in an OMS.
   - Update internal state (e.g., "step 2 complete, waiting on risk check").
   - Produce an intermediate or final report for a human.

   Actions may modify the environment (e.g., create an order) or simply add information that will influence later perception (e.g., computed Greeks).

The loop then repeats: the results of actions (tool outputs, order status, human feedback) feed the next perception step. A financial agent is therefore less like a single "smart query" and more like a continuously running process with memory, goals, and guardrails.

Core Components of an LLM Agent

To make this loop implementable, it is useful to think in terms of concrete components, many of which you saw in simplified form in earlier chapters:

Perception layer. Responsible for ingesting and preprocessing raw signals:

- Polling or subscribing to data feeds (market data, news).
- Querying internal systems (positions, risk, limits, user config).
- Normalizing and filtering data (e.g., sampling intraday ticks to avoid overload).
- Compressing data into a textual or structured summary suitable for the LLM.

State store. Tracks the *episode* of work the agent is currently engaged in:

- The high-level goal (e.g., "build and size a duration-neutral bond basket").
- Intermediate hypotheses (candidate instruments, rejected ideas).
- Status of subtasks (data fetched, risk checked, execution pending).
- Error flags and exceptions encountered so far.

State can live in memory for short-lived tasks or in a database for long-running workflows, which is crucial for audit and for resuming after failures.

LLM reasoner. The LLM itself, plus prompts and configuration:

- System prompt encoding role, policies, and overall objective.
- Task prompt describing the current step and available tools.
- Constraints on verbosity and detail (token budget).

This component generates candidate plans, arguments, or tool-call instructions given the perceived state.

Policy layer. A rule-based or learned component that constrains the model:

- Enforces risk and compliance rules (e.g., no shorting restricted names).
- Limits what tools can be used and with what parameters.
- Caps depth of loops and maximum capital usage.
- Decides when to escalate to a human instead of proceeding autonomously.

In regulated environments, the policy layer should be as explicit and interpretable as possible.

Tools and actions. The concrete operations the agent can perform:

- Data tools: fetch historical prices, fundamentals, risk factors.
- Analytics tools: compute VaR, Greeks, factor exposures, backtests.
- Execution tools: stage orders, simulate slippage, route to venues.
- Communication tools: send emails, populate dashboards, raise alerts.

In later sections we will go deeper on tool design; here they play the role of "muscles" that enact the intentions formed by the LLM.

Logging and audit. A persistent record of:

- Every state snapshot and relevant perception input.

- Every LLM call, including prompts and responses.
- Every tool invocation, with parameters and results.
- Final decisions and, if available, realized outcomes (e.g., trade P&L).

This is essential for compliance, debugging, and evaluating systematic performance over time.

Design Patterns for Control Loops

Within this overall architecture, different financial use cases call for different control-loop patterns. The main axes of variation are: how many steps the loop runs, what triggers each step, and how much autonomy the agent has.

Single-Step vs. Iterative Agents

Single-step agents. These wrap an LLM but run the loop only once. They are structurally similar to basic completions but embed more context and policy.

- **Example: Pre-trade analytics on demand.** A user requests: "Summarize key risk metrics for my `US_Equity_Growth` portfolio and highlight top 5 contributors." The agent:
    1. Perceives by fetching the portfolio holdings and current risk report.
    2. Reasons once to generate a textual summary and a concise table.
    3. Acts by returning the report to the user.

No iterative planning is needed. The control structure around the LLM ensures consistent data access, formatting, and logging, but the logical loop runs only a single time.

Iterative agents. These revisit perception and reasoning multiple times within one episode.

- **Example: Building a thematic basket.** Starting from a theme ("AI infrastructure beneficiaries"), the agent might:
    1. Propose an initial list of candidates and required data.
    2. Act to fetch fundamentals, factor exposures, and liquidity metrics.
    3. Perceive the new data and update its view.
    4. Reason about which names to keep or drop and how to size them.
    5. Call risk tools to compute portfolio-level exposures and limits.
    6. Possibly revise the basket again based on risk output.

Each cycle incrementally refines the solution. Iterative patterns are powerful but must be tightly controlled to avoid runaway loops and costs.

Reactive vs. Deliberative Agents

Agents also differ in how they respond to stimuli:

Reactive agents. These respond directly to events with minimal planning.

- **Example: Intraday news triage.** When a news feed delivers a new headline related to a watchlist name:
    1. Perception: ingest headline and current price move.
    2. Reasoning: quickly classify severity (e.g., "no action," "monitor," "urgent review").
    3. Action: send an alert or update a dashboard.

The agent's goal is to react quickly and consistently, not to run a long multi-step project.

Deliberative agents. These construct and follow plans over multiple steps.

- **Example: Overnight risk checks.** Every evening:

1. Perception: load end-of-day positions and risk reports.
2. Reasoning: plan a sequence of checks (limit breaches, concentration, stress scenarios).
3. Action: call tools to run each check, aggregate results, and draft a human-readable summary.
4. Repeat: if anomalies are found, loop back to gather more detail or propose mitigations.

Deliberative agents often benefit from explicit "planning prompts" that ask the LLM to lay out steps before taking actions.

Event-Driven vs. Scheduled Execution

Event-driven execution. The loop is triggered by external events:

- A price moves beyond a threshold.
- A new filing or earnings release is published.
- A human user submits a query or clicks a UI element.

The agent must be ready but idle most of the time; latency constraints can be tight. This pattern is common for intraday monitoring, alerts, and execution support.

Scheduled execution. The loop runs on a fixed schedule:

- Nightly end-of-day risk and compliance checks.
- Weekly factor-rotation analysis.
- Monthly performance attribution and client reporting.

Here the system can afford more computation per run, and it is easier to batch data access and logging.

In practice, many production systems blend these patterns: a scheduled overnight agent prepares a baseline risk report, and an event-driven intraday agent reacts to deviations from that baseline.

State Management and Serialization

Financial agents must not only act correctly but also leave a clear trail of *why* they acted as they did. This makes state management central rather than incidental.

What to store.

At a minimum, an episode's state should capture:

- The initial goal and user instructions.
- The sequence of perception inputs used (data snapshots, news items).
- All intermediate decisions and hypotheses (e.g., candidate baskets).
- The tools invoked and their parameters.
- Final actions taken (e.g., orders staged, reports emitted).

Serialization.

To support logging, replay, and audit, state should be serializable into a structured format (e.g., JSON or database rows). Practical guidelines:

- Assign each episode a unique ID and store step numbers.
- Separate raw data (e.g., full risk report) from summaries used in prompts.
- Redact or hash sensitive content where necessary, but preserve enough to reconstruct logic.
- Include timestamps for each step to enable latency and performance analysis.

This makes it possible to replay an episode offline, feeding the same perceptions to the agent and checking whether it behaves consistently under updated models or policies.

Engineering Constraints: Tokens, Latency, and Termination

The elegance of the perception–reasoning–action loop has to coexist with hard engineering limits.

Token budgeting.

Each LLM call consumes tokens for both input and output. In financial agents:

- Inputs can grow large if you naïvely include full portfolios or long histories.
- Outputs can grow large if you allow unconstrained reasoning or verbose explanations.

Control strategies include:

- Summarize and compress upstream: pre-aggregate portfolio risk into a small set of key metrics.
- Limit chain-of-thought verbosity: instruct the model to be concise and set maximum output length.
- Bound iterations: set explicit caps on step count and total tokens per episode.

Latency control.

Some tasks can tolerate minutes; others must respond in seconds or less. You can:

- Choose smaller or faster models for latency-critical steps.
- Pre-compute heavy analytics (e.g., daily factor exposures) and have the agent only retrieve them.
- Parallelize independent tool calls where possible.
- Set timeouts on steps, with fallback behaviors if a tool is slow or down.

Termination criteria.

An agent must know when to stop. Simple rules include:

- A maximum number of iterations or total tool calls.
- A convergence condition (e.g., portfolio risk within agreed bounds and no new violations found).
- An explicit "done" signal from the LLM, which the policy layer then validates.

If termination conditions are not met but limits are hit, the agent should degrade gracefully—produce a partial result, clearly mark it as incomplete, and notify a human.

Failure Modes and Safeguards

Without safeguards, agentic systems can fail in ways that are subtle and dangerous in a financial context.

Hallucinated tools and parameters.

The model may invent function names or use nonsensical arguments (e.g., negative quantities, unknown tickers). Mitigations:

- Validate all tool calls against a strict schema before execution.
- Maintain a whitelist of allowed tools for each agent role.
- Have the policy layer reject invalid calls and optionally ask the LLM to correct them.

Stuck or oscillating loops.

The agent might repeatedly call the same tools without making progress (e.g., alternately adding and removing the same names from a basket). Mitigations:

- Enforce step limits and detect repeated state patterns.

- Introduce explicit "reflection" prompts after several steps to ask the agent whether it is stuck and should stop or escalate.

Contradictory objectives.

Agents might implicitly optimize for conflicting goals (e.g., maximizing yield and minimizing duration while under tight liquidity constraints). Mitigations:

- Make objectives explicit and prioritize them in prompts and policy.
- Have the policy layer check for obvious conflicts (e.g., impossible constraints) and return a clear explanation instead of letting the agent thrash.

Risk and compliance breaches.

The most serious failures involve unauthorized exposures or actions. Here safeguards must be layered:

- Pre-trade checks at the policy layer for all execution-related actions.
- Hard limits in downstream systems (OMS, risk engines) that reject illegal orders even if the agent attempts them.
- Human-in-the-loop approval for sensitive categories (e.g., new strategies, large notional trades).

Putting It Together: Wrapping an LLM for Finance

To close this section, it is helpful to summarize what it means, in practical terms, to "wrap an LLM in a robust control structure" for finance:

1. **Define the role and scope.** Decide whether the agent is for research, risk, execution support, or governance, and articulate its responsibilities and limits.

2. **Specify the perception inputs.** Identify exactly which data sources and signals it can see, and how they will be summarized for the model.

3. **Design the state representation.** Choose what aspects of goals, intermediate steps, and errors you will track and serialize.

4. **Choose tools and actions.** Implement a small, safe set of tools tightly coupled to your infrastructure (data, analytics, OMS).

5. **Implement a policy layer.** Encode risk, compliance, and operational rules that vet all LLM proposals before they are enacted.

6. **Embed the perception–reasoning–action loop.** Orchestrate repeated steps where needed, with clear triggers and termination conditions.

7. **Instrument for cost and reliability.** Monitor tokens, latency, failures, and outcomes; use logs to refine prompts, tools, and policies over time.

In the next sections we will deepen two aspects of this picture. First, we will examine how to design and integrate tools and function calls so that agents become capable financial actors with controlled access to data and execution. Second, we will look at multi-agent architectures, where specialized agents (research, risk, execution, governance) coordinate through explicit planning and arbitration rather than a single monolithic loop.

4.2 Tool Integration and Function Calling

In the previous section we treated an agent as a control loop wrapped around an LLM: the agent perceives state, reasons about it, and takes actions. Up to this point, however, our "actions" have been somewhat abstract. In a real trading or research environment, an action means something concrete: fetching a time series, computing a risk measure, staging an order, or sending a report.

In this section we make that concrete by introducing *tools* and *function calling*. We will see how to turn a general-purpose language model into a capable market participant by wiring it to analytics libraries, data sources, and execution venues via safe, schemaed interfaces. We focus on the end-to-end pipeline: how the model selects and parameterizes tools, how arguments are validated against risk and compliance rules, how results flow back into the agent's state, and how to avoid dangerous or nonsensical calls.

From Text Generation to Tool-Using Agents

An LLM by itself only produces text. If you ask it:

> "What is the one-week at-the-money implied volatility for EURUSD?"

it will attempt to *guess* an answer based on its training data, but it does not have direct access to your pricing system. In a live trading context, this is unacceptable. What you want instead is:

- The model recognizes that this question requires live market data.
- It calls a well-defined function, such as get_fx_implied_vol.
- That function queries your pricing library or market data API.
- The result is returned to the model as structured data.
- The model uses that actual value in its explanation or downstream reasoning.

In other words, the LLM shifts from *answering directly* to *deciding which tools to use and how*. The accuracy and safety of the overall system now depend critically on how you design and govern those tools.

Schemaed Tools: Contracts Between Agent and Infrastructure

A **schemaed tool** is a function or API endpoint with a clear, machine-readable contract:

- A name that conveys intent (e.g., fetch_historical_prices, compute_portfolio_var).
- A set of input parameters with types, allowed values, and units.
- A structured output schema (e.g., JSON with typed fields).
- Documentation describing semantics, assumptions, and limitations.

When integrated with an LLM, this schema plays three roles:

- It tells the model *what it can do*. The prompt advertises available tools and their arguments.
- It allows the system to *validate* any proposed call before execution.
- It structures the response so that the agent can reason about the result in subsequent steps.

For financial tools, good schema design is especially important because mistakes can be costly. A few concrete guidelines:

Use constrained enums for venues and instruments.

Instead of asking the model for a free-text venue name, define something like:

- venue $\in$ {"XNYS", "XNAS", "ARCA"}
- asset_class $\in$ {"equity", "fx", "rates", "credit"}

This prevents hallucinated venues and makes it easier to apply venue-specific risk rules.

Make units and currencies explicit.

Financial quantities are unit-sensitive. For example:

- notional_ccy (e.g., "USD", "EUR").
- notional_amount (numeric, positive).
- price (numeric, in price_ccy).

If a tool expects an annualized volatility in percent, state that in the schema and validate that arguments fall in a plausible range.

Include mandatory risk parameters.

Any tool that can affect execution should force the LLM to specify risk-related arguments, such as:

- max_slippage_bps
- time_in_force (e.g., "DAY", "IOC")
- limit_price

This encourages the model to think in terms familiar to a trader and enables the policy layer to enforce firm-level constraints.

The Tool-Calling Pipeline

To understand how all this fits into the agentic loop, it is helpful to break down the tool-calling pipeline into distinct stages. We will keep to a simple but realistic scenario: an agent that computes a portfolio's factor exposures and checks them against limits before drafting a summary.

1. Prompting the Agent With Available Tools

At the start of a reasoning step, the system constructs a prompt that includes:

- The agent's current goal (e.g., "analyze this portfolio's factor exposures vs. limits").

- The current perception state (portfolio holdings, known limits).
- A description of available tools, each with name, purpose, and schema.

For example, the prompt might say in natural language:

> You can call compute_factor_exposures(portfolio_id, factor_model_name) to obtain current factor exposures, and check_exposure_limits(portfolio_id) to retrieve applicable limits and any existing breaches.

The LLM is then instructed to either:

- Respond directly in natural language, *or*
- Propose one or more tool calls in a specified structured format.

2. Model Selects Tool and Fills Arguments

Given this prompt, the model might produce something like:

> Call compute_factor_exposures with portfolio_id = "US_EQUITY_GROWTH" and factor_model_name = "HML_SMB_MKT".

or, in structured JSON form. The key is that the LLM is now using its understanding of the task to *choose* tools and parameters, rather than answering purely from memory.

3. Validation Against Schema and Risk Rules

Before this call touches any live system, the tool router and validator:

- Check that portfolio_id is a known portfolio and that the model is authorized to access it.
- Validate that factor_model_name is one of the allowed options.
- Enforce any role-based restrictions (e.g., research agent vs. execution agent).

If any check fails, the system does *not* execute the call. Instead it can:

- Return an error back to the LLM ("unknown portfolio ID") and ask for correction.
- Or escalate to a human, depending on the severity.

This validation step is non-negotiable in production systems. It prevents hallucinated or unauthorized interactions with sensitive data or trading venues.

4. Execution in Analytics or OMS Services

Once validated, the tool is executed by a deterministic service:

- Analytics tools run in risk engines, pricing libraries, or research databases.
- Execution tools talk to the OMS or simulated OMS, which enforces additional controls.

For our factor-exposure example, the analytics service might:

- Look up current holdings and factor betas.
- Compute portfolio-level exposures and standard errors.
- Return a structured object listing exposures by factor.

5. Result Injection Back Into Agent State

The tool's result is then:

- Logged for audit (tool name, arguments, result, timestamp).
- Inserted into the agent's state and the next prompt as structured data plus a short textual summary.

For example, the next LLM call might see:

> Factor exposures computed: {"MKT" = 1.1}, {"HML" = -0.3}, {"SMB" = 0.2}. Your equity risk policy specifies max absolute exposure of 0.25 on {"HML"}.

The agent can then reason about breaches and propose mitigation steps (e.g., reducing certain positions).

6. Natural-Language Reasoning and Further Tool Calls

With these results in context, the LLM:

- Interprets the numbers (e.g., "the portfolio is significantly underweight value (negative HML)").
- Decides whether to call further tools (e.g., a rebalancing optimizer).
- Or produces a human-readable explanation without further actions.

This interplay between tools and text is what elevates the agent beyond a static dashboard: the model can decide which analytics are relevant and explain them in domain-appropriate language.

End-to-End Flow: A Sequence Diagram

To anchor this pipeline, it is useful to visualize the message flow between the main components: the LLM agent, the tool router, the validator, the analytics or OMS service, and the logger.

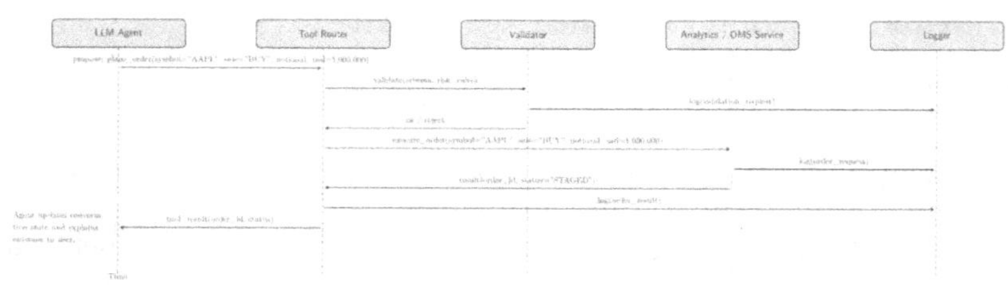

This sequence illustrates several important ideas:

- The agent never talks directly to the OMS; it always goes through a router and validator.
- Every step that matters for compliance (validation, order request, result) is logged.
- The final result returned to the agent is structured, so it can be used in further reasoning.

Examples of Financial Tools

To make tool design more concrete, consider a few common categories.

Data retrieval tools.

These provide access to time series and reference data, for example:

- fetch_historical_prices(symbol, start_date, end_date, interval)
- get_fundamentals(symbol, as_of_date)
- get_portfolio_holdings(portfolio_id, as_of_date)

Schemas here should:

- Constrain date formats and intervals (e.g., daily, hourly).
- Express missing data behavior (e.g., how corporate actions are handled).

Analytics tools.

These encapsulate heavy computations:

- compute_var(portfolio_id, horizon_days, confidence_level)
- run_factor_regression(symbol, factor_model_name, window_-days)
- compute_greeks(option_id, scenario)

For such tools, schemas need to:

- Enforce sensible ranges (e.g., confidence level between 0.9 and 0.999).
- Clarify model variants (e.g., historical vs. parametric VaR).
- Indicate performance characteristics (e.g., may take up to 5 seconds).

Risk and limit-check tools.

These help keep the agent within bounds:

- check_exposure_limits(portfolio_id)
- check_single_name_limits(symbol, proposed_notional, direction)
- simulate_stress_scenario(portfolio_id, scenario_name)

By making these tools first-class, you encourage the model to *ask permission* before suggesting aggressive trades.

Execution and OMS tools.

These are the most sensitive, because they can affect live orders:

- stage_order(symbol, side, quantity, limit_price, venue, time_in_force)
- cancel_order(order_id)
- get_order_status(order_id)

Here, design for safety:

- Separate tools for *simulation* (paper trading) from production.
- Require explicit flags for simulation vs. live (e.g., environment = "SIM").
- Have the OMS itself enforce credit and risk limits, independent of the agent.

Sandboxing, Determinism, and Backtesting

To build confidence in an agent, you will want to backtest or simulate its behavior on historical data. Tools play a key role here.

Simulation vs. production tools.

A practical pattern is to define twin sets of tools:

- *Simulation tools* that:
  - Read from historical data stores.
  - Use deterministic pricing and execution models.
  - Never touch live systems.
- *Production tools* that:
  - Use current market data and real OMS connections.
  - Are tightly guarded by validation and risk checks.

By swapping tool sets while keeping prompts and logic the same, you can replay agent decisions on past dates and evaluate how they would have performed.

Determinism and reproducibility.

Tools should behave as deterministically as possible, given the inputs and a reference data snapshot. This makes it feasible to:

- Reproduce historical runs for audit.
- Compare different model versions using the same tool outputs.
- Debug interactions between reasoning and analytics.

Where non-determinism is unavoidable (e.g., Monte Carlo VaR), you can fix random seeds or record simulation parameters.

Reducing Hallucinated or Unsafe Tool Calls

Even with good schemas, models can still propose odd or unsafe tool usage. Several patterns help reduce this risk.

Tool whitelists and role-specific views.

Do not expose every tool to every agent. For example:

- A research agent might see data and analytics tools, but no live execution tools.
- An execution-support agent might see only a limited set of staging and status tools.

Restricting visibility narrows the surface area for mistakes.

Explicit refusal behaviors.

When no tool is appropriate, the model should be encouraged to say so. Prompt it with instructions such as:

> If the user asks you to do something that requires tools you do not have, or that violates risk or compliance rules, you must refuse and explain why.

This is particularly important when users might try to push agents beyond their scope.

Out-of-band sanity checks.

For certain critical tools, you can implement automatic sanity checks on outputs:

- Validate that order sizes and notional amounts are within predefined ranges.
- Check that computed metrics (e.g., volatility, spreads) fall within plausible intervals.

If a tool's output looks implausible, the agent can discard it, flag an error, and avoid making decisions on suspect data.

Bringing It Back to the Agent Loop

If we step back, integrating tools and function calling changes the agent's perception–reasoning–action loop in three important ways:

- **Perception** now includes not only raw data feeds but also the *results of previous tool calls*. The agent can build up a richer view of the world over multiple steps.
- **Reasoning** is no longer just text prediction; it includes deciding which tools to call, in what order, and with what parameters, subject to schema and policy constraints.
- **Action** becomes concrete and auditable: each step corresponds to calls to well-defined services or to generating human-facing outputs.

A well-designed set of schemaed tools effectively defines the "action space" of your financial agent. By choosing this space carefully and wrapping it in validation, logging, and risk controls, you can allow LLM-based agents to participate meaningfully in research and trading workflows without giving them unbounded power.

In the next section we will move from single agents to *multi-agent* systems, where specialized agents—for research, risk, execution, and governance—coordinate with one another. The tool integration concepts introduced here will carry over: each agent will have its own tool set, and orchestration will consist largely of routing tasks and information among them in a controlled way.

4.3 Multi-agent Coordination and Planning

In the previous sections we treated an agent as a single LLM-centric loop, wired to tools and wrapped in policies. That is a good mental model for many focused tasks: summarizing risk, triaging news, or staging a small order. But realistic financial workflows often cut across multiple domains of expertise and responsibility. The person who designs a strategy is not the same as the person who signs off on its risk, nor the same as the trader who decides how to slice and route orders.

In this section we extend the agentic view from *one* agent to *systems of agents*. We will see how to decompose complex financial tasks across specialized roles—Research, Risk, Execution, Governance—and how to orchestrate them using explicit planning, delegation, and arbitration. The goal is to design architectures where agents collaborate productively without creating chaotic "chatter loops" or violating risk and compliance boundaries.

Why Multi-agent Systems for Finance?

A single, powerful agent *could* in principle do everything: ingest data, generate trade ideas, run risk, optimize execution, and write governance reports. In practice, there are good reasons not to centralize all of these functions in one monolithic agent:

- **Separation of concerns.** Financial institutions already separate research, risk, trading, and compliance. Reflecting this in agent design aligns with existing controls.
- **Diverse tool sets.** Each role uses different tools: research relies on data and analytics, risk on stress testing, execution on OMS and smart order routing, governance on policy and logging.
- **Different objectives and constraints.** A research agent maximizes insight and creativity, while a risk agent is explicitly conservative and adversarial.
- **Scalability and maintainability.** Smaller, focused agents are easier to test, monitor, and evolve than a single "do everything" system.

Multi-agent systems allow you to mirror institutional structure in software: specialized agents play to their strengths, while orchestration logic ensures that their outputs compose into coherent end-to-end workflows.

Core Roles in a Financial Multi-agent System

Let us start by defining four prototypical agent roles that appear repeatedly in trading and investment workflows.

Research Agent.

Focused on idea generation and analysis. Typical responsibilities:

- Scan news, filings, and alternative data for themes and signals.
- Propose trade hypotheses (e.g., "AI infrastructure beneficiaries," "value-growth spread compression").
- Construct candidate baskets or strategies, using analytics tools for backtesting and factor analysis.
- Produce research notes and rationales understandable to humans and other agents.

Risk Agent.

Acts as a critical counterparty to Research and Execution:

- Compute risk metrics (VaR, stress losses, factor exposures).
- Check concentration, liquidity, and mandate-specific constraints.
- Suggest hedges or alternative constructions that reduce undesired risk.
- Veto or flag proposals that violate firm-level or client-level policies.

Execution Agent.

Specializes in translating approved strategies into concrete orders:

- Design order-slicing and routing plans given liquidity and market conditions.
- Simulate impact and slippage for proposed orders.

- Stage and monitor orders through the OMS, respecting risk and credit limits.
- Feed back execution quality metrics (e.g., implementation shortfall, VWAP vs. benchmark).

Governance Agent.

Ensures transparency, compliance, and accountability:

- Enforce firm policies on what classes of strategies are allowed.
- Ensure required approvals (e.g., human sign-off) are collected.
- Maintain an audit trail linking decisions, data, and outcomes.
- Periodically review agent behavior for drift or anomalies.

These roles do not need to be implemented as separate physical services from day one, but they are useful conceptual building blocks: they define boundaries of responsibility and tool access.

Coordinator-Worker and Blackboard Patterns

How do these agents collaborate? Two fundamental orchestration patterns are particularly useful in finance.

Coordinator-worker pattern.

A central **Planner** (or Coordinator) receives a high-level task, decomposes it into subtasks, and assigns each to the appropriate specialized agent. It then integrates the results into a coherent outcome.

For example, given the objective "build and size a thematic basket for AI infrastructure and propose an execution plan," the Planner might:

1. Ask the Research Agent to propose candidate names and rationales.
2. Ask the Risk Agent to analyze exposures and apply limits.
3. Ask the Execution Agent to design an order plan for the approved basket.

4. Ask the Governance Agent to check that the overall proposal complies with policies.

Blackboard pattern.

Instead of direct point-to-point messaging, agents communicate via a shared **blackboard**: a structured workspace where they post artifacts (candidate baskets, risk reports, execution plans) and read what others have written. The Planner may still exist, but agents can also react to updates: for instance, the Risk Agent might automatically analyze any new basket posted by Research.

In practice, many systems combine these ideas: a Planner orchestrates the main steps, while a shared state store (the "blackboard") holds intermediate results and metadata.

Right after introducing these patterns, it is helpful to visualize the architecture of a multi-agent financial system.

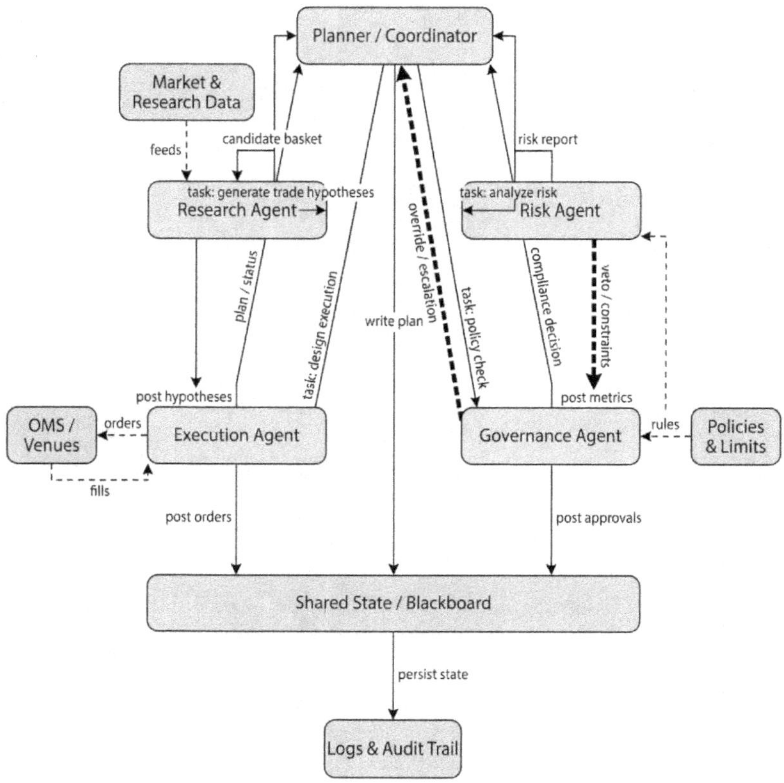

Explicit Planning: Turning a Goal into a Workflow

At the heart of multi-agent coordination is planning: mapping a high-level objective into a sequence (or graph) of subtasks, each assigned to an appropriate agent.

Step-by-step plans.

For relatively linear tasks, the Planner can construct a simple numbered plan, for example:

1. Ask Research to propose a thematic basket of 20–40 U.S. equities exposed to AI infrastructure.

2. Ask Risk to compute factor exposures, liquidity, and stress tests.
3. If Risk finds violations, send feedback to Research to revise the basket.
4. Once risk-approved, ask Execution to design an implementation plan with target schedule and venues.
5. Ask Governance to review the full package and either approve or request changes.

This plan is itself a piece of state written to the blackboard. Each agent, when invoked, can see which step it is fulfilling and what upstream context exists.

Dependency graphs.

More complex workflows are not purely linear. Some steps can run in parallel; others depend on multiple predecessors. The Planner can represent this as a dependency graph:

- Research and a data-quality agent might both run early: one generating ideas, the other checking data integrity.
- Risk analysis might wait until both have completed.
- Execution design may depend on both risk output and a liquidity forecast.

Although we will not draw explicit graph notation here, it is useful to think in these terms: the Planner schedules subtasks when their inputs are available, and recomputes parts of the graph when upstream results change.

Iterative refinement.

Importantly, planning is not a one-shot affair. In practice:

- Risk may reject the first version of a basket for concentration or liquidity reasons.
- Execution may highlight impractical order sizes or venues.

- Governance may flag policy issues with the strategy description.

The Planner must be able to loop:

1. Aggregate feedback from Risk, Execution, and Governance.
2. Decide what changes are needed (e.g., "reduce small-cap names," "avoid certain sectors").
3. Send a revision request to Research with specific constraints.

This is multi-agent analog of the iterative control loops you saw in single-agent settings: except now the "steps" are interactions between agents, not just between an agent and tools.

Delegation: Assigning Work to Specialized Agents

Given a plan, delegation is the act of turning a subtask into an agent invocation.

Defining subtask interfaces.

Each agent should expose a clear interface describing:

- Inputs it expects (e.g., "basket definition and constraints" for Risk).
- Outputs it will produce (e.g., "risk metrics and pass/fail decision").
- Side effects it may trigger (e.g., writing to logs, updating blackboard).

These interfaces allow the Planner to treat agents as composable building blocks.

Context packaging.

When the Planner delegates, it must package the right context:

- For Research: theme description, universe constraints, and any prior risk feedback.

- For Risk: current candidate basket, relevant limits, and applicable scenarios.
- For Execution: approved target basket, risk notes, and market conditions.
- For Governance: the entire history of the episode, including rationales and risk sign-offs.

This is analogous to tool-calling: instead of calling a pricing function, the Planner calls an agent by constructing an appropriate prompt and data bundle.

Handling incomplete or ambiguous outputs.

Agents may return partial or uncertain results. For example:

- The Research Agent might say: "I am unsure about 3 of these names due to limited liquidity data."
- The Risk Agent might say: "VaR is within limits, but stress scenario X is borderline."

The Planner's job is to interpret such responses and decide whether to:

- Request refinement from the same agent.
- Involve another agent (e.g., a data-quality or liquidity agent).
- Escalate to a human supervisor.

Arbitration and Conflict Resolution

In a non-trivial system, agents will sometimes disagree. A Research Agent might love a trade that the Risk Agent dislikes; an Execution Agent might find that a theoretically optimal plan is not executable in current markets.

Rule-based hierarchies.

One straightforward approach is to define hierarchies:

- Risk can veto proposals that breach limits; its "no" is binding unless overridden by a human.
- Governance can override all agents when policies are at stake.
- Execution can request adjustments but not alter the target risk profile unilaterally.

The Planner encodes and enforces these rules. For example, if Risk returns $\text{decision} = \text{"REJECT"}$, the Planner does *not* send the basket to Execution, but instead routes feedback back to Research.

Voting and consensus.

For some decisions, especially in research contexts, you may create multiple competing agents and use a voting scheme:

- Several Research Agents, each using different data or models, propose trade ideas.
- A Meta-Research or Governance Agent aggregates, scores, and selects those with broad support.

This can increase robustness but comes with the risk of more complex interactions. Clear rules about how votes are weighted and what constitutes consensus are important.

Human-in-the-loop escalation.

Certain conflicts should always surface to a human:

- Persistent disagreement between Risk and Research on a large or novel strategy.
- Situations involving unusual market stress where models may be unreliable.
- Any policy or regulatory grey areas.

The Governance Agent can monitor for such patterns (e.g., repeated vetoes or exceptions) and trigger escalation workflows: compose a summary of the disagreement and send it to a designated human approver.

Concrete Multi-agent Workflows

To make these ideas more tangible, consider three concrete workflows.

Earnings-season monitoring.

1. Research Agent monitors calendar and news, flagging important upcoming earnings for portfolios.
2. For each name, it posts a brief "earnings preview" to the blackboard.
3. Risk Agent reviews exposures around each event, running scenario analyses for large positions.
4. If risk is elevated, Execution Agent designs possible hedging or de-risking trades.
5. Governance Agent ensures that any changes are consistent with mandates and that required approvals are logged.

Here orchestration ensures that every major earnings event triggers a coordinated response rather than ad hoc, isolated actions.

Cross-asset hedging.

1. Research Agent detects that a large equity position is exposed to a macro factor (e.g., rates).
2. Risk Agent quantifies this exposure and suggests potential hedges across futures, swaps, or options.
3. Execution Agent evaluates liquidity and costs in candidate hedging instruments and proposes an implementation plan.
4. Governance Agent checks that the hedge is consistent with policy (e.g., allowed instruments and leverage).

The Planner coordinates these agents to avoid local optimizations (e.g., a hedge that looks good in isolation but conflicts with other portfolio-level constraints).

Automated report generation.

1. Research Agent drafts narrative for a client or internal report (performance drivers, notable trades).
2. Risk Agent contributes a section on risk evolution, breaches, and remediation.
3. Execution Agent contributes execution-quality metrics.
4. Governance Agent checks that disclosures meet regulatory requirements and that sensitive information is handled appropriately.

Multiple agents contribute sections to a single artifact. The Planner orchestrates the sequence (e.g., risk numbers must be finalized before narratives referencing them are frozen) and assembles the final document.

Operational Considerations and Complexity Management

Multi-agent systems can be powerful but also fragile if not carefully managed.

Avoiding agent "chatter" loops.

If two agents read from the same blackboard and trigger on each other's updates, they can enter a loop:

- Research posts a basket; Risk posts feedback; Research reacts and posts a minor change; Risk reruns analysis; and so on without convergence.

Mitigations include:

- Step counters and convergence criteria (e.g., stop after N_{iter} iterations or when risk metrics change below a threshold).
- Planner-mediated updates: only the Planner decides when to send feedback vs. when to terminate a refinement cycle.

Bounding system complexity.

As you add agents, the number of possible interactions grows. To keep complexity manageable:

- Limit the number of agents per workflow; start with a small set of core roles.
- Define clear interfaces and avoid "back channels" where agents bypass the Planner.
- Use consistent patterns for delegation and response to make behavior predictable.

Stable interfaces for extensibility.

Design agent interfaces so that new agents can be added or removed without breaking others:

- Use versioned schemas for blackboard entries (e.g., a standard format for "basket proposal" or "risk report").
- Have the Planner route tasks based on declared capabilities (e.g., "any agent that can handle 'risk_analysis' can be plugged in").

This helps you evolve the system incrementally: you might swap in a more advanced Risk Agent without changing the Planner logic.

Multi-agent coordination and planning extend the agentic paradigm from individual reasoning loops to institution-scale workflows. By decomposing tasks across specialized agents—Research, Risk, Execution, Governance—and orchestrating them with a Planner and shared state, you can:

- Reflect real organizational structures and controls.
- Combine diverse tools and objectives in a structured way.
- Resolve conflicts via clear hierarchies, voting, and escalation.
- Keep the system auditable and evolvable over time.

The next section will focus on the operational spine that makes such systems robust in production: memory, budgeting, and control. There we will examine how to manage agent memory across episodes, how to meter computational and capital usage, and how to implement guardrails and monitoring so that multi-agent systems remain efficient, compliant, and trustworthy in live trading and research environments.

4.4 Memory, Budgeting, and Operational Control

The previous sections treated agents primarily as intelligent decision-makers: they perceive state, reason, call tools, and coordinate with other agents. To move from prototypes to production, however, we must confront a more mundane but essential question: *how do we keep these systems under control over time?*

In a live trading or research environment, an agent is not just a clever function. It is a long-running service that:

- Accumulates knowledge across episodes and days.
- Consumes scarce resources: tokens, compute, engineer time, and ultimately capital.
- Operates under hard legal and compliance constraints.

This section develops the "operational spine" of agentic systems: memory, budgeting, and guardrails. We will see how to give agents usable memory without drowning them in context, how to meter both computational and financial budgets, and how to wrap their behavior in policy layers that keep them safe, auditable, and fit for regulated environments.

What We Mean by Memory in Agents

In human terms, "memory" is one thing. For agents, it is useful to distinguish several layers.

Short-term conversational state

This is the working memory of an agent during a single *episode* or task:

- The user's initial request and clarifications.
- The agent's own intermediate steps and hypotheses.
- Tool outputs and derived summaries.

In earlier sections we represented this as the agent's *state store*: a structured object that the control loop updates each time it perceives, reasons, and acts. Short-term state typically lives:

- In RAM or a fast key-value store.
- Within the model's current context window as a textual summary.

It disappears once the episode ends, except insofar as it has been serialized to logs.

Longer-horizon episodic memory

Beyond a single episode, you often want agents to remember:

- Past research artifacts: previous baskets, backtests, and rationales.
- Historical trades and their outcomes: P&L, risk behavior, execution quality.
- Known preferences and constraints of specific users or portfolios.

This is akin to an "experience database." It should not just be raw logs; it must be structured enough for efficient retrieval. Typical implementations use:

- Relational or document databases for structured information (trades, limits, reports).

- Vector stores for semantically indexed text (research notes, discussions).

Shared institutional memory

In multi-agent systems, some memories are *shared*:

- A central repository of policies and procedures.
- Standard templates for risk reports and client communications.
- Canonical definitions of factor models, scenarios, and benchmarks.

All agents should see a consistent view of such institutional knowledge. This is naturally housed in knowledge bases or document repositories, accessed via retrieval-augmented generation (RAG) techniques.

Designing Memory for Agents: Patterns and Trade-offs

Memory is not simply about saving everything. In fact, saving too much can make an agent worse, by overwhelming its context window and slowing down reasoning. A good design carefully balances richness and cost.

What to store during an episode

From an operational perspective, each episode should be logged with enough detail to:

- Reconstruct why the agent acted as it did (for audit).
- Diagnose failures and guide improvements (for debugging).
- Allow partial reuse of work (for efficiency).

Practical guidelines:

- **Store inputs, not just outputs.** Save key perception inputs: which data snapshots, news items, and limits the agent considered.

- **Record decisions and rationales.** If the agent chooses basket A over basket B, log that reasoning in structured form where possible.
- **Record tool calls.** For each call, store the tool name, parameters, result, and timing.

This information forms an "episode trace," which is distinct from the conversational context fed to the model at each step.

Summarization and distillation

Not every detail from every episode needs to live in long-term memory. Instead, you can:

- Summarize episodes at the end into compact "experience cards":
  - What was the task?
  - What were the key decisions?
  - What went well or badly?
- Store these summaries in a vector store indexed by:
  - Symbols, portfolios, and strategies involved.
  - Risk profiles and scenarios.
  - User, date, and outcome metrics.

Later, when a similar task arises, the agent can retrieve a small number of relevant past episodes, inject them into its context, and reason analogically: "Previously, when building an AI infrastructure basket under similar constraints, these patterns worked well; here is how we might adapt them."

Retrieval prompts that avoid context bloat

Retrieval can easily flood the context if not controlled. An effective pattern is:

- Use a retrieval layer (outside the LLM) to fetch candidate memories.

- Apply filters: relevance, recency, and importance (e.g., large P&L impact).
- Summarize top candidates further if they are still too long.
- Present only a handful of distilled examples in the prompt, with clear labels.

Prompts should explicitly tell the model how to use retrieved memory:

> You are building a new thematic basket. Below are summaries of three similar past baskets and their outcomes. Use them as examples, but adapt to the current constraints; do not blindly copy.

This keeps the agent grounded without overwhelming it.

Budgeting Computational Resources

Tokens and compute are direct costs of operating LLM agents. Without metering and budgets, a promising prototype can quietly become an expensive liability.

Token tracking and limits

At minimum, you should track:

- Tokens per model call (prompt and completion).
- Tokens per episode.
- Tokens per user, portfolio, or business unit over time.

This enables several controls:

- **Per-call caps.** Set maximum input and output token limits; truncate or summarize when needed.
- **Per-episode budgets.** For example, "no more than 30,000 tokens for nightly risk checks on portfolio X."

- **Per-tenant quotas.** Allocate budgets across teams to prevent a single workflow from consuming all resources.

The agent's prompts should be written with these limits in mind: ask for concise reasoning when appropriate, and favor structured outputs over long narratives.

Model selection and latency budgets

Different tasks have different latency and quality requirements:

- Intraday execution support may require sub-second responses and can tolerate less elaborate reasoning.
- Overnight research tasks can accept higher latency in exchange for richer analysis.

Budgeting here involves:

- Choosing model sizes and types per task (e.g., a smaller, faster model for filtering, a larger model for final synthesis).
- Imposing wall-clock limits per step and per episode.
- Designing timeouts and fallback strategies:
  - Use cached analytics if live computation exceeds a threshold.
  - Return a partial answer with a clear flag when time runs out.

These choices can be codified in the policy layer so that the agent cannot, for example, accidentally call an expensive foundation model in a latency-critical loop.

Capital and Risk Budgets for Agents

Beyond computational resources, agents in trading contexts must be constrained by financial budgets.

Capital envelopes

A simple but effective metaphor is a *capital envelope*: each agent, or set of agents, is allocated:

- A maximum gross or net exposure.
- A maximum notional per symbol or asset class.
- A maximum leverage ratio.

These numbers can be dynamic (changing with market conditions or over time), but they provide a hard ceiling. An Execution Agent might be allowed to:

- Stage orders that, if fully filled, keep exposures within the envelope.
- Suggest trades beyond the envelope only in "simulation" mode, clearly labeled as hypothetical.

Risk-budget-based constraints

More sophisticated frameworks base budgets on risk metrics:

- Value-at-Risk (VaR) or Expected Shortfall limits.
- Factor exposure bands (e.g., HML exposure between -0.2 and 0.2).
- Stress-test loss thresholds for specific scenarios.

In this design:

- The Risk Agent computes current and projected metrics for proposed trades.
- Budgets are expressed in those terms (e.g., "incremental 1-day 99% VaR must not exceed $2m").
- The policy layer enforces that no execution tools can be called for proposals that would exceed risk budgets.

This keeps agents' behavior aligned with firm-wide risk appetite rather than only raw notional constraints.

Guardrails and Policy Layers

Guardrails are the mechanisms that translate regulations, firm policies, and best practices into enforceable constraints.

Pre- and post-trade checks

For actions related to trading, two main guardrail points are:

Pre-trade. Before staging or routing an order, the system should:

- Check symbol-level restrictions (sanctioned entities, restricted lists).
- Validate that trade direction and size are permissible under mandates.
- Confirm that capital and risk budgets are not breached.

If any check fails, the agent should not be able to proceed. Ideally, the OMS itself enforces these rules in addition to the agent's policy layer, creating defense in depth.

Post-trade. After execution:

- Update exposures and risk metrics promptly.
- Log the linkage from decision rationale to actual orders and fills.
- Trigger any required post-trade surveillance or analysis.

This allows later investigators to trace a clear chain: from high-level strategy rationale down to individual fills.

Prompt and action filters

Agents can also be constrained at the language level:

- **Prompt filters** screen user inputs for prohibited requests (e.g., asking the agent to circumvent rules) before they ever reach the LLM.
- **Action filters** analyze the model's proposed actions (tool calls, narratives) for policy violations before execution or delivery.

For example, an action filter could prevent an agent from generating client-facing text that makes promises about guaranteed returns, or that references internal confidential information.

Human approval workflows

For sensitive tasks, automatic guardrails are not enough; human approval is required. Agents can:

- Prepare a full package: data, rationale, risk analysis, and proposed actions.
- Send it to a designated approver (e.g., risk manager, portfolio manager).
- Wait for an explicit approval or rejection, which may come with comments.

The agent then acts (or does not) based on that decision, and records the approval in its logs. This pattern is especially important for:

- New strategy launches.
- Large trades or changes in risk profile.
- Exceptions to standard policies.

Monitoring, Dashboards, and Drift Detection

Once agents are running regularly, you need continuous visibility into their behavior, not just isolated audits.

Operational metrics

Useful metrics include:

- Number of episodes, per agent and per business line.
- Average and tail latency per step and per episode.
- Token and compute usage over time.
- Tool-call frequencies and error rates.

Dashboards that expose these metrics help you spot anomalies: sudden spikes in usage, rising error rates for a particular tool, or abnormally long-running episodes.

Behavioral and outcome metrics

Beyond mechanics, you should also monitor:

- Distribution of proposed and executed trades by asset class, region, and liquidity.
- Risk metrics pre- and post-agent actions (e.g., did the agent tend to increase or decrease VaR?).
- Execution quality related to agent-proposed strategies.

These metrics enable:

- Detection of drift: if an agent's behavior changes significantly after a model or prompt update.
- Comparative evaluation: across agent versions or strategies.

Incident analysis and post-mortems

When something goes wrong (e.g., an unexpected risk spike or an operational failure), you want to perform a structured post-mortem. This relies on:

- Rich episode logs and state traces (as discussed under memory).
- Links between tools, agents, and external systems.
- Clear time-stamping and versioning of models, prompts, and policies.

A good practice is to feed lessons from post-mortems back into:

- Policy updates (tightening or clarifying guardrails).
- Prompt and tool design (better instructions, additional checks).
- Training data for future models or evaluators.

Putting It All Together

- **Memory** gives agents context beyond a single prompt: recent episode state, relevant historical experience, and shared institutional knowledge. It must be structured, retrievable, and bounded to avoid overwhelming reasoning.
- **Budgeting** ensures that agents use computational and financial resources responsibly: tracking tokens, latency, and capital; setting per-task and per-tenant limits; and enforcing them in the policy layer.
- **Operational control** wraps agents in guardrails: pre- and post-trade checks, prompt and action filters, human approval workflows, and continuous monitoring. These controls transform clever prototypes into systems that regulators and risk committees can live with.

In practice, building production-ready agentic systems for finance is less about ever-more-sophisticated models and more about disciplined engineering around them. By treating memory, budgets, and guardrails as first-class design elements, you can create agents that are not only intelligent, but also efficient, predictable, and trustworthy participants in your research and trading workflows.

Chapter 5

Evaluation, MLOps, and Governance

Most generative-AI finance projects fail not because the ideas are bad, but because no one can answer three simple questions: Does it work, can we ship it safely, and who is accountable when it doesn't? This chapter tackles those questions head-on. You'll learn how to evaluate LLMs and agents against financial tasks that actually matter, simulate their trading impact before risking capital, wire them into production-grade MLOps pipelines, and wrap them in the guardrails of risk management, compliance, and security. The goal is simple: move from impressive demos to systems you can trust with real money-and explain with a straight face to your CIO, your risk committee, and your regulator.

5.1 LLM and Agent Evaluation

In the earlier chapters we focused on how to build generative models and agentic workflows that can read financial text, call tools, and support research and trading decisions. The natural next question is: *how do we know they are any good?* In a trading or investment organization, "good" is not an abstract notion. It must connect directly to profit and loss (PnL), risk, operational cost, and compliance.

This section develops a practical framework for evaluating LLMs and agents in finance. We will:

- Define a simple taxonomy of agent tasks (research, broker/chat, portfolio and execution support, workflow orchestration).
- Map each task type to appropriate evaluation methods and metrics.
- Show how to tie these metrics back to financial impact: alpha, risk, slippage, analyst-hours, and cost per decision.
- Explain how evaluation results become gates for promotion from research to staging to production environments.

Throughout, the emphasis is on grounded, finance-specific benchmarks rather than generic language benchmarks or toy tasks.

From Language Quality to Financial Impact

A common mistake when adopting LLMs in finance is to rely on general-purpose metrics such as BLEU scores, win rates on open-domain leaderboards, or human ratings of "fluency." These can be loosely correlated with quality, but they do not tell you whether:

- The agent preserved the numbers and units in a 10-K excerpt.
- A portfolio recommendation respects your risk limits and constraints.
- An execution suggestion decreased or increased realized trading costs.
- A research summary actually changed an analyst's decision or saved measurable time.

To move beyond this, we need to make the evaluation question much more concrete:

> For a specific financial workflow, what does success look like in terms of PnL, risk, and cost, and what intermediate behaviors must the agent exhibit to get there?

This leads naturally to a task-centric view of evaluation.

Task Taxonomy for Financial Agents

Most LLM and agent use cases in finance fall into a handful of recurring patterns. Having a clear taxonomy helps structure evaluation.

- **Research summarization and analysis**
  - Examples: summarizing earnings calls; extracting KPIs from filings; comparing two issuers' capital structures; preparing investment memos.
  - Outputs: structured fields (numbers, labels) and narrative analysis.
- **Broker, client, and internal chat**
  - Examples: answering client questions about positions and performance; explaining product features; responding to internal queries about risk reports.
  - Outputs: compliant, accurate, and concise natural language.
- **Portfolio recommendation and rebalancing support**
  - Examples: suggesting rebalancing moves; proposing hedges; ranking trade ideas given risk budgets.
  - Outputs: action proposals (e.g., trades, weight changes) with supporting rationale.
- **Execution decision support**
  - Examples: choosing between VWAP and POV algorithms; suggesting urgency adjustments; routing to venues based on liquidity.

- Outputs: orders, execution parameters, or recommendations to a trader or OMS.

- **Workflow orchestration**
  - Examples: orchestrating calls to pricing models, risk engines, and data vendors; scheduling and logging periodic reports; escalating exceptions to humans.
  - Outputs: sequences of tool calls, data transformations, and escalations.

Each task type has a different notion of correctness and a different link to business outcomes. A universal metric is neither realistic nor desirable. Instead, we create evaluation suites tailored to each task.

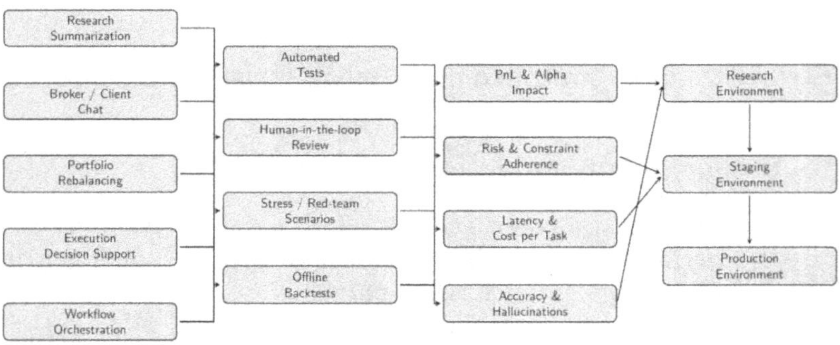

Designing Evaluation Suites: Methods and Metrics

For each task type, we design an evaluation suite that combines automated checks with human judgment and, where possible, historical data. The suite should cover at least four dimensions:

- **Accuracy and extraction fidelity**: are facts, numbers, and references correct?
- **Constraint satisfaction**: does the agent respect risk limits, portfolio rules, and compliance policies?

- **Operational performance**: what are latency, throughput, failure rates, and cost per task?
- **Business impact**: how does the agent influence PnL, volatility, drawdowns, slippage, and labor costs?

We now step through these dimensions in a financial context.

Accuracy and Extraction Fidelity

For research and data-extraction tasks, accuracy is not just about being "roughly right." Small numerical errors can have large consequences.

Reference-grounded checks. When the agent cites a filing, news article, or data table, we can automatically verify that:

- The referenced document actually contains the quoted figure or statement.
- The numerical value and units are preserved (e.g., $1.2 bn is not turned into $1.2 m).
- Date and period references are correct (Q2 2023 vs. FY 2023).

In a RAG setting, this often means comparing the agent's extracted fields against a trusted parser or a labeled dataset. The metric might be simple extraction accuracy, or a weighted accuracy where misreading an EPS figure is penalized more heavily than mislabeling a segment name.

Financial correctness severity. Not all errors are equal. For finance, we often categorize mistakes by *materiality*:

- **Critical**: errors that would likely change an investment decision (wrong revenue growth, reversed sign on cash flows).
- **Moderate**: errors that create confusion or extra work but do not change the decision (minor rounding differences).
- **Minor**: cosmetic issues (typos, slightly awkward phrasing).

Human evaluators tag errors with these severity labels. Over time, you can summarize the system with metrics like "critical error rate per 100 tasks," which is much more meaningful for risk than a raw accuracy score.

Constraint Satisfaction and Risk Alignment

Agents that suggest trades or portfolios must operate under explicit constraints: position limits, sector caps, leverage bounds, liquidity requirements, regulatory rules, and internal risk policies.

Static constraint checks. For each recommendation, you can compute:

- Percentage of suggestions that violate hard constraints (e.g., shorting a restricted stock, exceeding a sector cap).
- Average and maximum deviation from soft constraints (e.g., recommended risk slightly above target).

These can be implemented as automated tests: feed the agent synthetic portfolios and instructions, then run its outputs through a constraint-checking engine. The result is a constraint violation rate and distribution.

Risk profile comparison. For portfolio-level decisions, we compare the risk metrics of agent-suggested portfolios to benchmarks:

- Changes in volatility, maximum drawdown, VaR, or tracking error relative to a baseline.
- Concentration metrics such as Herfindahl index, top-10 positions, or sector exposures.

These comparisons can be run on historical data to avoid live risk-taking, forming part of the offline evaluation.

Operational Performance and Cost

Even a well-behaved agent can be unusable if it is slow, unstable, or too expensive.

Latency and reliability. Core metrics include:

- End-to-end response time distributions (p50, p95, p99).

- Tool call success rates and timeout rates.
- Escalation rates to human agents when the LLM refuses or fails.

Different tasks demand different service-level objectives (SLOs). Execution support might require sub-second or low-single-digit-second latency; an in-depth research memo can tolerate longer runtimes.

Cost per decision. Token usage, external API fees, and compute costs should be translated into cost per task:

- Average and distribution of cost per research memo, per client chat session, or per rebalancing run.
- Cost decomposition: LLM inference vs. tool calls vs. overhead.

These can be benchmarked against human baselines (e.g., analyst-hours saved) and against alternative model configurations (smaller models, more caching, fewer tool calls).

Business and PnL Impact

Ultimately, the point of introducing LLMs and agents is to create value. Depending on the use case, "value" can mean:

- Incremental alpha (e.g., better timing around news events).
- Reduced trading costs (e.g., improved execution quality, lower market impact).
- Improved risk outcomes (e.g., fewer constraint breaches, smoother drawdowns).
- Increased capacity (e.g., more coverage per analyst, faster client turnaround).

These are often assessed via *offline proxies* and then confirmed in controlled live experiments:

- **Offline proxies**: backtesting signals generated from historical documents; simulating execution strategies with historical order book data; replaying prior client chats and measuring quality and time-to-resolution.

- **Live A/B testing**: comparing desks or time windows with and without the agent, holding other conditions as constant as possible.

Not every system directly trades, but nearly every system ultimately connects to PnL, risk, or cost through some chain. Making that chain explicit is crucial for governance.

Finance-Specific Grounding Checks

Finance adds several domain-specific failure modes that generic LLM evaluation rarely covers. You should construct targeted tests for each.

Ticker and Instrument Sanity

LLMs are prone to hallucinating tickers or confusing similar ones. Tests should include:

- Asking about nonexistent tickers and verifying the agent either refuses or says "unknown."
- Presenting ambiguous names (e.g., "Apple") without tickers and checking whether the agent clarifies which entity is meant.
- Ensuring mapping from ticker to legal entity and currency is correct.

Metrics include hallucinated ticker rate and ambiguity-handling quality, which can be graded by humans.

Time Horizon and Regime Awareness

Misunderstanding time horizons is especially dangerous in trading. Evaluation prompts should stress:

- Differentiation between intraday, short-term swing, and long-horizon investment recommendations.
- Appropriate references to historical periods (e.g., not using 2024 data when asked to reason as of 2018).

Test cases should include adversarial prompts such as "As of 2018, would you buy this stock given these filings?" with only pre-2018 data available. Any use of future information is a look-ahead violation.

Units, Currencies, and Scaling

Converting units incorrectly (bps vs. percent, millions vs. billions) can break risk and PnL calculations. Evaluation datasets should deliberately mix:

- Dollar, euro, and local-currency amounts.
- Different units for spreads and returns (basis points vs. percentages).
- Notional and per-share figures.

Automated tests then verify that transformations and reasoning preserve correct scaling and units.

Stress Testing and Red-Teaming for Finance

A robust evaluation regime should expose agents to adversarial and unusual scenarios, not only "happy paths."

Ambiguous and Conflicting Instructions

In practice, users will issue messy instructions. Stress tests should include:

- Conflicting constraints (e.g., "Max 5% in any stock" and "Allocate 20% to stock A").
- Vague time horizons ("Is this a good stock?") which require the agent to ask clarifying questions.
- Overly optimistic or aggressive risk instructions that conflict with firm policy.

We measure whether the agent:

- Identifies the conflict or vagueness.

- Requests clarification or defers to policy.
- Avoids making overconfident recommendations.

Model and Tool Degradation Scenarios

Agents depend on tools (pricing services, risk engines, market data feeds). Evaluation should simulate:

- Tool timeouts or corrupted responses.
- Stale data (e.g., delayed prices).
- Downgraded LLM quality (smaller, cheaper models).

Metrics include safe-failure behavior: does the agent surface the incident, fall back to conservative defaults, or stop and escalate?

Connecting Evaluation to Environments and Promotion

Evaluation is most powerful when it drives deployment decisions. We can think in terms of three environments:

- **Research** Fast experimentation with loose constraints.
- **Staging** Controlled environment mirroring production systems, but without real-money impact.
- **Production** Live use with real trades, clients, or regulatory consequences.

Each environment has associated acceptance criteria, drawing on the metrics above.

Research Environment: Feasibility and Basic Safety

In research, you explore ideas and measure whether they are promising:

- Accuracy and extraction fidelity on curated datasets.

- Basic constraint satisfaction on synthetic scenarios.
- Rough estimates of latency and cost.

Promotion from research to staging might require:

- Critical error rate below a threshold on held-out test sets.
- Zero violations of specified hard constraints in automated tests.
- Latency and cost within broad but acceptable bands.

Staging Environment: Stability and Impact Proxies

In staging, you integrate with real data pipelines and systems:

- Run offline backtests for portfolio and execution agents.
- Re-play past client or internal chats to simulate live volume.
- Measure operational metrics (throughput, failure rates, escalations).

Promotion from staging to production might require:

- Offline PnL and risk metrics at least as good as a baseline (or within a small tolerance if the goal is cost reduction rather than alpha).
- Stability of latency and error rates over a representative time window.
- Successful completion of stress and degradation scenarios.

Production Environment: Guardrails and Feedback

In production, evaluation shifts towards continuous monitoring and feedback loops (covered in detail in the MLOps section of this chapter). For the purposes of evaluation design, we define:

- Ongoing SLOs and alerts for latency, cost per task, and error rates.

- Sampling strategies for human post-hoc review of critical tasks.
- Logging and tagging of outcomes (e.g., "trade executed," "recommendation overridden by risk," "client complaint") to feed back into datasets.

Agents that breach thresholds (e.g., sudden spike in hallucinated ticker rate, or unexpected rise in constraint violations) trigger predefined rollback procedures.

Human-in-the-Loop Evaluation in Finance

Because many financial tasks are high stakes and context-dependent, purely automated evaluation is insufficient. Human-in-the-loop review plays at least three roles:

- **Labeling complex outcomes** that cannot be easily captured in rules, such as whether a research summary is "decision-ready" or whether a client response is appropriately nuanced.
- **Calibrating materiality**, by tagging which errors matter for PnL or risk.
- **Discovering new failure modes**, through qualitative observation and incident reports.

To keep this process manageable:

- Sample tasks based on risk: review a high proportion of high-impact decisions (e.g., trade recommendations) and a smaller sample of low-impact tasks.
- Use structured rubrics: evaluators assign scores or labels for accuracy, risk alignment, compliance, and clarity.
- Store evaluations as structured data: they become part of your evaluation corpus for future model comparisons.

Putting It All Together

The goal of this section has been to turn "Is our AI any good?" into a series of concrete, measurable questions directly tied to PnL, risk, and cost. The key steps are:

- Classify each agent use case into a clear task type.
- For each task, define evaluation suites combining automated metrics, human judgment, and, where applicable, historical backtests.
- Incorporate finance-specific grounding checks on tickers, time horizons, units, and constraints.
- Design stress tests and red-team scenarios that reflect real-world edge cases and failures.
- Tie evaluation metrics to environment-specific promotion criteria, so only well-evaluated agents reach production.

In the next section, we will deepen the connection between agent decisions and market outcomes by building explicit backtests and simulations. That will allow you to test how these evaluated agents would have behaved under historical market conditions, with realistic frictions, before they ever touch real capital.

5.2 Backtesting and Market Simulation

In the previous section we focused on *evaluating* LLM and agent behavior at the level of tasks: accuracy on filings, adherence to constraints, latency, and cost per decision. That gave us a static picture of quality. For trading and portfolio applications, however, what ultimately matters is how those decisions would have behaved in real markets.

Backtesting and market simulation are the bridge between micro-level evaluation and macro-level PnL and risk. In this section we develop that bridge for LLM-driven agents. We will:

- Distinguish event-driven and bar-based backtests and show how agents fit into each.
- Build data pipelines that avoid classic backtest biases and respect information timing.
- Incorporate realistic transaction costs and frictions, including those affected by LLM behavior.
- Use walk-forward and rolling-window evaluation to avoid overfitting prompts and tools.
- Tie everything back into documentation and governance for deployment decisions.

The goal is to estimate, as honestly as possible, what would have happened if your LLM-based agent had been running in historical markets.

Where Agents Plug into Backtests

Traditional systematic strategies map numerical features of the market (prices, volumes, fundamentals) into trading signals. LLM-based agents introduce a new layer: they transform *textual and conversational* information into decisions.

To backtest such systems, we must clarify where the agent sits in the trading pipeline. Two patterns are common.

Bar-Based Backtests with LLM-Generated Signals

In a **bar-based** backtest, you work with time bars: daily, hourly, or minute-by-minute candles. At each bar you have:

- Market data: open, high, low, close, volume.
- Possibly fundamental or derived data: factors, analyst estimates, risk metrics.
- For LLM agents, additional features derived from text: news, filings, transcripts, and internal notes.

An LLM-driven research or trading agent in this context typically does one of the following:

- Reads new textual events since the last bar (earnings, macro releases, firm news).
- Produces a signal such as “positive/negative/neutral” or a score in $[-1, 1]$ for each asset.
- Passes that signal into a traditional portfolio construction or execution engine.

The backtest engine then simulates portfolio holdings and PnL as if the LLM-derived signals had been available in real time.

Event-Driven Simulators for Execution Agents

In an **event-driven** backtest, the simulator reacts to discrete events rather than fixed time bars. Events include:

- Order arrivals and modifications.
- Trades in the market (tape updates, order book changes).
- News flashes or internal alerts.

LLM-based *execution agents* fit naturally here. For example, the agent might:

- Observe the live order book and recent trade history.
- Read a stream of short news headlines.
- Decide whether to speed up or slow down a parent order, switch algorithms, or route to a different venue.

Backtesting such an agent requires an order book simulator or historical level-2 data. The environment feeds events to the agent and simulates how its actions would have affected execution prices, slippage, and market impact.

Data Pipelines: Avoiding Bias and Preserving Timing

Before you can backtest, you must construct a data pipeline that presents the agent with exactly the information it would have had at each point in the past. This is harder with text than with prices, but the principles are the same.

Survivorship Bias and Universe Definition

Survivorship bias arises when you define your backtest universe using only current constituents, ignoring delisted or bankrupted firms. LLM-based strategies are vulnerable to the same issue.

To avoid it:

- Use historical index constituent lists or a security master that includes delisted names.
- Ensure that textual data (filings, news) for dead companies are still included.
- For cross-sectional strategies, define the tradable universe at each point in time, not retroactively.

If a research agent that reads 10-Ks would have avoided certain bankruptcies, that can only be evaluated if those filings are actually present in your dataset.

Look-Ahead Bias and Timestamp Alignment

Look-ahead bias occurs when the agent, even indirectly, sees information that was not yet available at the decision time. With text, this can happen in subtle ways:

- Using a cleaned "final" version of a filing that was amended later.
- Treating a news article's publication date incorrectly (e.g., in local vs. UTC time).
- Including a full-day batch of events when the decision should be made intraday.

To protect against this:

- Store and use precise timestamps for each document or message.
- Define a clear decision schedule (e.g., "agent runs at 15:30 UTC using all documents timestamped before 15:00 UTC").
- When simulating intraday decisions, align event timestamps to the simulator clock and process them sequentially.

A helpful mental model is: at each backtest step, you take a snapshot of "what the world looked like to the agent at that moment" and no more.

Data Snooping and Prompt Overfitting

LLMs and agents can be tuned using prompts, tool choices, and examples. If you choose these by trial and error on the full historical period, you risk **data snooping**: effectively learning the noise in the data.

To mitigate this, we will later introduce walk-forward and rolling-window procedures. For now, simply note that your backtest dataset must be partitioned carefully into development and evaluation segments, just as you would for any machine learning model.

Transaction Costs and Market Frictions

Any serious backtest must include *transaction costs*: commissions, bid-ask spreads, market impact, and other frictions. LLM-based agents can change *how much* and *how often* you trade, so cost modeling becomes even more important.

Basic Cost Components

A simple but useful transaction cost model might include:

- **Explicit costs**: broker commissions and fees per share or per trade.
- **Spread costs**: half the bid-ask spread times the absolute traded volume.
- **Market impact**: an additional penalty that grows nonlinearly with trade size relative to average daily volume (ADV).

- **Financing and borrow**: for leveraged or short positions, borrowing costs and locate fees.

For each simulated trade, the engine deducts these costs from PnL. Over time, you can compare the *gross* and *net* equity curves to understand how much of the apparent edge disappears after frictions.

How LLM Behavior Affects Costs

LLM agents can influence trading costs in several distinctive ways:

- **Increased trading around news**: A news-reading agent might react quickly and frequently to textual events, increasing turnover.
- **Different order types**: An execution agent might prefer more aggressive orders in high-conviction situations or more passive orders otherwise.
- **Venue selection**: The agent may route to alternative venues or dark pools based on its reading of market conditions.

Your backtest should reflect these behaviors. For instance, if the agent decides between market and limit orders, the simulator should use different cost assumptions for each, potentially including missed fills or partial executions for passive orders.

Walk-Forward and Rolling-Window Evaluation

In the previous evaluation section, we highlighted the risk of overfitting prompts and tools to historical data. Backtesting is where that risk becomes most acute.

Walk-Forward Evaluation

Walk-forward evaluation mimics how the system would be developed and used in reality:

1. Choose an initial *training window* (e.g., 3 years of history).
2. Within that window, design and tune:

- Prompt templates and instructions.
- Tool configurations and accessible analytics.
- Risk caps and constraint parameters.

3. Freeze the configuration and run the agent forward on the next *out-of-sample* period (e.g., the next 6 months).
4. Record performance metrics.
5. Roll the window forward and repeat: expand or slide the training period, retune if realistic, and test on the next period.

This produces a series of out-of-sample performance segments, which can be stitched together to form a more honest equity curve. At no point does the agent "peek" at the future when being tuned.

Rolling-Window Stability Checks

Beyond walk-forward, you can evaluate the *stability* of performance across different subperiods:

- Crisis vs. calm periods.
- High- vs. low-volatility regimes.
- Bull vs. bear markets; different rate environments.

For each window, you compute key metrics (annualized return, volatility, Sharpe, max drawdown, turnover, cost percentage). Large swings in these measures might indicate that the agent leans heavily on conditions that may not persist.

Regime-Sensitive Analysis and LLM-Specific Effects

LLM agents often shine in particular market regimes: for example, news-heavy environments where textual information is abundant. To understand this, you can segment your backtest into regimes based on:

- Volatility (e.g., VIX levels or realized volatility).

- Event intensity (e.g., number of news headlines or filings per day).

- Macro conditions (e.g., rising vs. falling rate environments).

For each regime, compare the LLM-driven strategy to a traditional baseline that does not use text or agents. Look for:

- Periods where both perform similarly (LLM adds little).

- Periods where the LLM strategy diverges—positively or negatively—and analyze why.

- Relationships between regime variables and incremental alpha or cost.

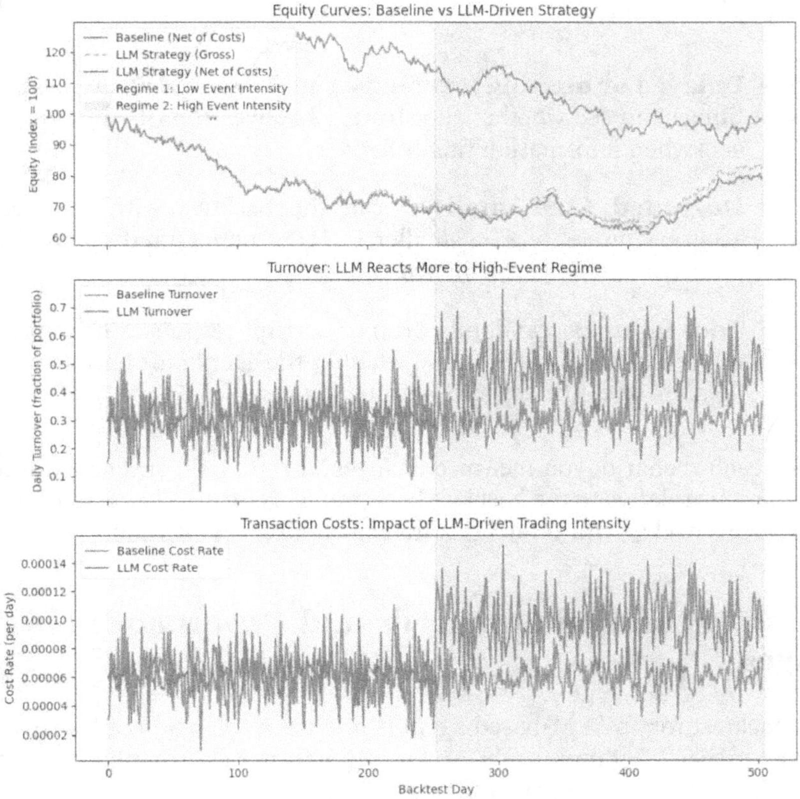

This kind of visualization helps you see how an LLM-based strategy's increased trading around news or events might generate gross alpha but also higher turnover and costs, which can erode net performance, particularly in certain regimes.

Scenario Tests and Partial Failures

Beyond historical replay, you should consider *scenario tests*: controlled distortions of the environment that explore how the agent behaves under stress or partial failure, complementing the red-team approach in the earlier evaluation section.

Examples include:

- **Delayed or missing text feeds**: simulate late news or missing filings and see whether the strategy behaves robustly or overreacts when information finally arrives.
- **Degraded LLM quality**: run the backtest with a lower-accuracy model (e.g., a smaller LLM) to understand sensitivity of PnL to model performance.
- **Tool failures**: randomly drop or corrupt responses from pricing or risk tools and observe whether the agent falls back to safe defaults or continues as if nothing happened.

For each scenario, you measure changes in PnL, risk, and constraint violations relative to the baseline backtest. This forms a key part of the evidence package for model risk management and governance.

Documentation Standards and Governance Linkages

A backtest for an LLM-based agent is not just a collection of charts; it is an artifact that must withstand scrutiny from risk, compliance, and audit teams. Good documentation typically covers:

- **Intended use**: what decisions the agent can and cannot make, and in which markets or products.
- **Data sources and timing**: how textual and numerical data were collected, timestamped, and filtered.
- **Assumptions and limitations**: including approximations in transaction-cost models, coverage gaps in text, and any simplifications in order book simulation.
- **Evaluation methodology**: details of walk-forward and rolling-window procedures, choice of benchmarks, and regime definitions.

- **Sensitivity analyses**: how performance changes when you adjust key parameters, such as cost assumptions, holding periods, or prompt variants.
- **Stress and scenario results**: how the agent behaves under delayed data, degraded models, or extreme market moves.

These elements feed directly into the governance process described later in the chapter. For example, a firm might require that any agent influencing exposures above a threshold notional must:

- Demonstrate robust performance over at least one full market cycle.
- Show stable risk metrics across multiple regimes.
- Pass predefined scenario and stress tests.

From Backtest to Production Playbook

Finally, it is helpful to think of your backtesting and simulation framework as a *rehearsal space* for production. The same components—data feeds, execution simulators, risk engines, and logging—will later appear in live systems. A good playbook typically includes:

1. **Prototype in research**: connect your agent to a historical data store and basic backtest engine, focusing on correctness and bias avoidance.
2. **Harden in staging**: run the same agent against high-fidelity simulations and historical replays that mirror production infrastructure.
3. **Shadow in production**: let the agent propose trades or actions in real time while a human or existing system actually executes, and compare the outcomes.
4. **Gradual activation**: only after satisfactory shadow performance and additional governance review does the agent begin to influence real orders or portfolios, initially under tight limits.

At each step, the backtest and simulation results serve as quantitative evidence for promotion, tying back to the evaluation metrics and acceptance criteria defined earlier in the chapter.

Backtesting and market simulation for LLM-driven agents extend classic quant techniques to a new class of decision-makers. The principles remain familiar:

- Respect information timing and avoid survivorship and look-ahead biases.
- Incorporate realistic costs and frictions.
- Use walk-forward and regime-based evaluation to guard against overfitting.
- Stress test agents under adverse and degraded conditions.
- Document assumptions and results to support governance and deployment decisions.

What is new is the need to connect rich, unstructured information and complex agent behavior to these simulations. Once you do, you gain a powerful lens on how your LLM-based research and trading agents would have behaved in real markets—before risking a single dollar of live capital.

5.3 MLOps, Deployment, and Monitoring

The first two sections of this chapter answered the questions "Is the agent *any good*?" and "How would it have behaved in past markets?" Evaluation and backtesting, however, are still laboratory activities. In practice, value is only created when LLM and agent systems run reliably inside live trading and research workflows.

This section explains how to move from the lab to production using concepts from MLOps-continuous integration and deployment (CI/CD), model and prompt registries, and observability-adapted to the specifics of generative AI in finance. The objective is simple to state but hard to achieve:

> Ship LLM and agent changes safely, with predictable behavior, bounded cost, and measurable performance, and be able to roll back when things go wrong.

We will proceed in four steps:

1. Outline a reference architecture for LLM and agent MLOps in a financial institution.
2. Show how CI/CD pipelines enforce tests, evaluation, and safety checks before deployment.
3. Describe observability geared to agents: not just latency and errors, but also semantic and business signals.
4. Close with monitoring-driven feedback loops, controlled rollout strategies, and rollback plans.

A Reference Architecture for LLM and Agent MLOps

Compared to traditional quant models, LLM-based agents introduce new moving parts: prompts, tools, routing logic, and conversation state. A clear architecture is essential to avoid "prompt spaghetti" and manual, ad-hoc deployments.

A practical architecture has four main layers:

1. **Data and features**: market data, text corpora, knowledge bases, and feature stores.
2. **Models and prompts**: base LLMs (internal or external), fine-tuned variants, prompt templates, and routing rules.
3. **Tools and agents**: pricing and risk engines, data APIs, order management interfaces, and the agent workflows that orchestrate them.

4. **Monitoring and feedback**: logging, metrics dashboards, alerting systems, and feedback channels from users.

Each layer spans three environments:

- **Research**: Fast iteration, weaker guarantees, small groups of users.
- **Staging**: Production-like infrastructure and data, but no direct impact on real trades or clients.
- **Production**: Live use under strict controls, with full audit and governance.

Crucially, we treat not only models but also prompts, tool definitions, and agent graphs as *versioned artifacts*. They must be traceable and reproducible in the same way as traditional code and models.

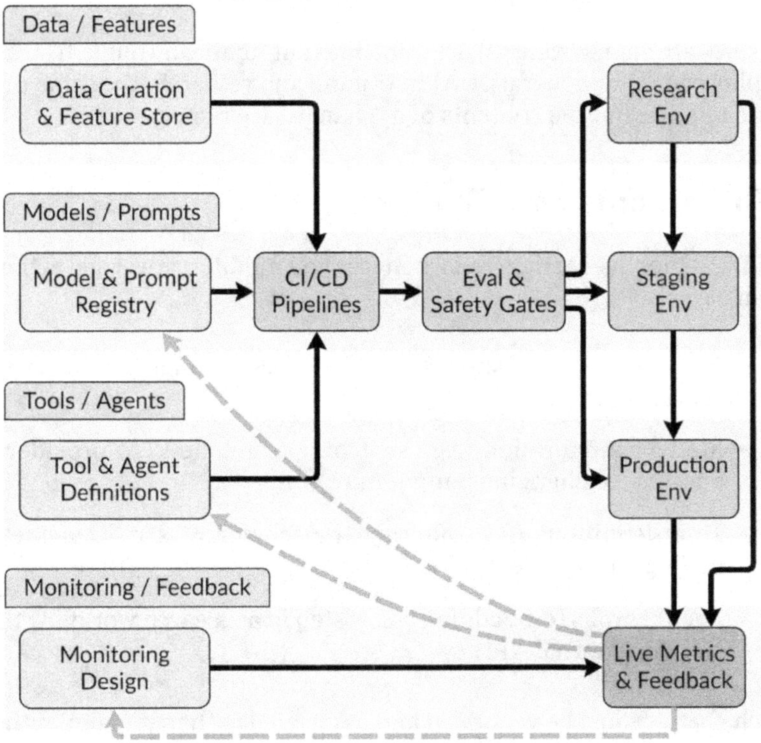

This pipeline-style diagram emphasizes two ideas that are particularly important in finance:

- Changes to prompts or tools are treated like code: they flow through CI/CD and evaluation gates, not directly into production.
- Monitoring is not an afterthought; it is wired into the pipeline with explicit feedback loops to model and agent design.

CI/CD for LLM and Agent Systems

In software engineering, CI/CD pipelines automatically build, test, and deploy code. For generative AI in trading and research, the same principle applies, but the contents of a "change" are richer.

What Counts as a Change?

A CI/CD pipeline is triggered whenever you modify a governed artifact, such as:

- Prompt templates and routing logic (e.g., changing instructions for risk limits).
- Model configuration (e.g., switching from one LLM provider to another, or changing temperature).
- Tool definitions (e.g., altering the schema of a risk engine or adding a new order type).
- Agent graphs (e.g., adding a new step in a research workflow that calls an external API).

Each change must be versioned and associated with metadata: author, timestamp, description, and links to tickets or approval records where appropriate.

Pipeline Stages

A typical CI/CD pipeline for LLM agents has several stages:

1. Static checks and unit tests.

These are fast, deterministic checks that run on every change:

- Prompt and config validation (e.g., required fields present, no malformed JSON).
- Tool schema compatibility (e.g., arguments still match the expected contract).

- Simple unit tests for agent flows: given a canned input, does the agent call the right tools in the right order?

2. Offline evaluation and regression tests.

Next, the pipeline runs the *offline evaluation suites* and *backtests* developed in earlier sections:

- Accuracy and constraint-satisfaction tests on curated datasets.
- Backtests or historical replays for trading and execution agents.
- Red-team and stress-test scenarios for edge cases.

Results are compared against baselines. You can encode policies such as:

- "Critical error rate must not increase."
- "Net PnL over the walk-forward backtest must not drop by more than X% unless explicitly allowed for a cost-reduction objective."
- "No increase in risk limit violations in synthetic tests."

3. Safety and policy checks.

Especially in regulated environments, automated checks for policy compliance are essential:

- Scan prompts and examples for banned phrases or instructions (e.g., guaranteeing returns).
- Ensure tools that can move money or place trades are only callable from approved agent flows.
- Validate that logging and audit requirements are preserved.

These checks can be partly implemented with rules and, in some cases, assisted by secondary LLMs acting as policy reviewers.

4. Deployment to environments.

If all checks pass, the pipeline can automatically:

- Deploy to *research* for exploratory users.
- Deploy to *staging* with production-like data and interfaces for further validation.
- Prepare a *candidate* for production deployment, often gated by manual approvals from model risk or product owners.

Each deployment records which versions of models, prompts, tools, and code are active. This provenance is critical for later investigations or audits.

Model and Prompt Registries

Traditional machine learning systems often use a *model registry* to track versions, metadata, and deployment status of models. For agentic LLM systems, you extend this idea.

What to Register

At a minimum, you should register:

- LLM models: identifiers, providers, training data summaries, performance benchmarks, and cost characteristics.
- Fine-tuned models or adapters: training datasets, objectives, and evaluation results.
- Prompt templates: full text, parameters (temperature, max tokens), and intended use.
- Tools: input/output schemas, documentation, and safety constraints (e.g., "max order size 10% ADV").
- Agent workflows: graph structures (nodes and edges), allowed tools at each node, and high-level descriptions of the task and risk level.

Each registry entry is assigned a unique version and linked to evaluation artifacts and backtests.

Why It Matters

A well-maintained registry enables you to answer concrete questions that come up frequently in finance:

- "Which prompt and model combination generated this particular trade recommendation?"
- "What changed between version 3 and version 4 of the research assistant, and how did evaluation metrics differ?"
- "Which workflows are currently permitted to access the live order management system?"

Without this traceability, diagnosing incidents or satisfying model risk management requirements becomes nearly impossible.

Observability for Generative AI in Finance

Once agents are live, you need good *observability*: continuous visibility into how they behave and what they cost. For LLM systems, observability spans three levels:

1. **Infrastructure metrics**: latency, availability, error rates.
2. **Interaction metrics**: prompts, tool calls, refusal rates, conversation lengths.
3. **Outcome metrics**: business and risk outcomes tied to each interaction.

Infrastructure Metrics

These are familiar from any production system:

- End-to-end response time (p50, p95, p99).
- Error and timeout rates for LLM and tool calls.

- Throughput: requests per second or per minute by desk, product, or user group.

You set SLOs for these metrics; for example, "95% of execution-support responses under 2 seconds." Breaches trigger alerts and may cause automatic throttling or downgrading to simpler flows.

Interaction and Semantic Metrics

Generative systems require richer signals about how they are being used:

- Distribution of task types (e.g., "research summary," "client query," "rebalance suggestion").
- Prompt length and complexity, which can affect both latency and cost.
- Tool-call patterns: which tools are being called, in what sequence, and how often they fail.
- Refusal vs. completion rates: how often the agent declines to answer or escalates.

Capturing these as structured logs (rather than only free text) lets you analyze behavior trends over time and across desks.

Outcome and Business Metrics

Finally, you should capture how each interaction ties into business outcomes. Examples include:

- For research agents: whether the analyst accepted the recommendation, modified it, or rejected it.
- For trading agents: whether the suggested trade was executed, overridden by risk, or modified by a trader.

- For client-facing chatbots: client satisfaction ratings, follow-up actions, and any complaints.
- For all workflows: tags for critical incidents, such as “incorrect data,” “constraint violation,” or “compliance escalation.”

These tags can be added by users through simple feedback interfaces or by downstream systems (e.g., risk engines flagging a violation). They become invaluable training and evaluation data for future iterations.

Cost Control as a First-Class Objective

LLM-based systems introduce a new operational risk: variable and sometimes substantial inference cost. In trading environments with high query volumes, careless design can produce large, unplanned bills.

Measuring Cost

You should measure:

- Token usage per request, broken down by prompt and completion.
- Cost per tool call for external APIs.
- Aggregate spend per desk, team, or application.

These metrics are monitored like any other production KPI. Sudden spikes in usage or cost trigger alerts, which can indicate either genuine demand growth or bugs (e.g., runaway loops in agent workflows).

Controlling Cost

There are several levers for cost control:

- **Model routing**: use cheaper models for low-risk, high-volume tasks and reserve premium models for complex or high-stakes decisions.

- **Caching**: store and reuse responses for repeated queries (e.g., static information about a product or historical filing summaries).
- **Prompt optimization**: trim unnecessary context, encourage concise answers, and avoid overly long system messages.
- **Budgets and quotas**: enforce per-tenant ceilings on daily or monthly usage, with soft and hard limits.

In finance, it is often useful to translate LLM costs into a per-task or per-analyst basis and compare them to human labor and infrastructure costs. This keeps discussions grounded in economics rather than raw token counts.

Monitoring-Driven Feedback Loops

Monitoring is not just about catching problems; it is a continuous source of data for improving agents.

Capturing Feedback and Incidents

Design your systems so that users and downstream checks can easily provide structured feedback:

- Simple buttons or tags: “useful,” “partially useful,” “incorrect,” “unsafe.”
- Free-text comments that can later be mined for common issues.
- Automatic incident tagging when a risk engine or compliance system flags a problem.

Each feedback item references the full context: model and prompt version, tools used, input data, and environment.

Feeding Back into Evaluation and Design

Regularly, you can:

- Aggregate feedback to identify the most common failure modes.
- Add representative examples to your evaluation datasets and red-team suites.
- Adjust prompts, routing logic, or tool access to reduce error-prone behaviors.

Importantly, these changes again flow through CI/CD and offline evaluation before they affect production. The loop is:

1. Production monitoring surfaces issues.
2. Issues are converted into test cases and prompts in research.
3. Changes are made and evaluated.
4. Successful changes are redeployed, and monitoring verifies improvement.

Rollout Strategies and Rollback Plans

Because LLM and agent behavior is complex, you should avoid "big bang" deployments. Instead, borrow from modern software practices:

Canary and Shadow Deployments

- **Canary**: deploy a new version to a small fraction of traffic (e.g., one desk or a subset of users) while the majority continues using the previous version. Compare key metrics and only ramp up if performance is stable.
- **Shadow**: run the new agent in parallel with the current system, but keep it read-only. It observes live inputs and generates recommendations, which are logged but not acted upon. This is particularly valuable for trading agents, where you can compare suggested trades to actual ones without risk.

Defining Rollback Criteria

Before deployment, decide what constitutes a failure that triggers rollback:

- Breach of latency or error-rate SLOs for a specified period.
- Increase in critical incident rate beyond a threshold.
- Material deterioration in backtested-like performance proxies (e.g., simulated transaction cost metrics from shadow trades).

Rollbacks should be automated where possible: revert to the previous registry version and configuration, update routing, and continue logging for diagnosis.

MLOps for LLM and agent systems in finance is about bringing the same discipline you apply to trading code to a richer, more flexible class of models. The key practices are:

- Treat prompts, tools, and workflows as versioned artifacts, governed alongside models and code.
- Use CI/CD pipelines to enforce static checks, offline evaluation, and safety gates before any change reaches production.
- Implement observability that spans infrastructure, interaction, and business outcome metrics, with cost treated as a first-class concern.
- Build monitoring-driven feedback loops that turn production experience into improved evaluation suites and better designs.
- Roll out cautiously with canary and shadow deployments, and define clear rollback criteria upfront.

With these foundations in place, generative AI agents can be integrated into research and trading systems as reliable, auditable components-subject to the same controls and standards as any other critical infrastructure in your firm.

5.4 Risk Management, Compliance, and Security

The previous sections established how to evaluate agents, backtest them realistically, and operate them in production using disciplined MLOps. In a financial institution, however, "working" is not enough. Any system that can influence trades, portfolios, or client communications must sit inside a robust framework of model risk governance, compliance controls, and security defenses.

This section explains how to wrap generative-AI systems in that framework so they can withstand internal challenge and regulatory scrutiny. We will:

- Show how to treat LLMs, prompts, tools, and workflows as governed models under model risk management (MRM).
- Connect agent activities to regulatory and firm policies on suitability, best execution, research independence, and client treatment.
- Describe security and privacy measures tailored to LLMs, including defenses against prompt injection and data leakage.
- Outline incident response practices that tie back into evaluation and MLOps processes.

Throughout, the theme is integration: agents become first-class citizens in the existing risk and control environment, not experimental side projects.

Model Risk Governance for LLM and Agent Systems

Most mid- to large-size financial institutions already maintain a formal model risk management framework, often guided by supervisory expectations. Generative-AI systems must fit into this framework, but they require extending some traditional concepts.

Defining the Model Inventory

Start by explicitly cataloging all relevant components in a *model inventory*. For LLM-based systems, entries may include:

- **Base LLMs**: vendor, architecture class, training corpus description, known limitations.
- **Fine-tuned models or adapters**: objectives, training data sources (e.g., research notes, chat transcripts), and evaluation results.
- **Embedding models** used in retrieval or similarity search.
- **Prompts and routing logic**: key templates, system messages, and task-specific instructions that materially affect behavior.
- **Tools and calculators**: pricing and risk engines, order management interfaces, data APIs, and internal microservices callable by the agent.
- **Agent workflows**: orchestrations that define how the system moves from inputs (documents, chats) to outputs (recommendations, orders, reports).

For governance purposes, each entry should specify:

- Intended use and scope (which products, markets, processes).
- Impact category or criticality (e.g., can it place trades, or is it advisory only?).
- Owners (business, technology, and model-risk contacts).
- Links to evaluation, backtesting, and monitoring artifacts from prior sections of this chapter.

A common pattern is to treat the entire *agent workflow* as a governed model, with LLMs, prompts, and tools recorded as submodels or components.

Validation and Approval of Agent Systems

Once in the inventory, a system typically undergoes *model validation* before significant use. For LLM agents, validation should cover:

Conceptual soundness.

Validators confirm that the overall design makes sense for its purpose:

- Are inputs, tools, and decision logic appropriate for the stated use case?
- Are constraints, risk limits, and policies encoded clearly and enforced mechanically where possible?
- Does the system avoid using data or signals in ways that would violate regulatory expectations (e.g., inappropriate use of confidential information)?

Empirical evidence.

Here, the evaluation and backtesting machinery you built earlier is brought forward as evidence:

- Static evaluation metrics: extraction accuracy, constraint satisfaction, critical error rates.
- Backtests and historical replays: PnL, risk, and cost performance under realistic frictions.
- Stress and scenario tests: behavior under delayed data, degraded models, and extreme markets.

Model risk reviewers are typically less interested in marginal benchmark gains and more focused on robustness, stability, and clear limitations.

Limitations and conditions of use.

Every model has boundaries. For LLM agents, documentation should spell out:

- Markets, instruments, or client types for which the agent *is not* approved.

- Conditions under which it must defer to humans (e.g., complex derivatives, very illiquid names, or large notional trades).
- Known weaknesses (e.g., less reliable on non-English texts, limited understanding of certain local regulations).

Approval is then granted for specific use cases, often with volume limits or trial periods, and linked to monitoring requirements.

Ongoing Model Risk Monitoring

Governance does not stop at approval. LLM-based agents should be subject to *ongoing model risk monitoring*, which reuses many of the monitoring metrics from the MLOps section but interprets them through a risk lens:

- Track incident rates and severity: constraint violations, incorrect outputs, or compliance escalations per 1,000 interactions.
- Monitor drift in input distributions (e.g., new types of documents) and output behavior.
- Periodically re-run evaluation suites and backtests, especially after major market regime changes or LLM updates.

Material performance shifts, new failure modes, or expansion into new use cases may trigger re-validation and potential changes in approval status.

Compliance: Embedding Policy into Agent Workflows

Regulatory and internal compliance requirements shape how agents can be used and what they can say or do. The key is to weave these requirements into *workflow design* rather than relying solely on after-the-fact reviews.

Record-Keeping and Auditability

Most financial regulations emphasize record-keeping and traceability. For agent systems, this implies:

- Logging prompts, responses, tool calls, and key intermediate decisions, with timestamps and user identifiers.
- Linking each material recommendation or action (e.g., a trade) to the exact model and prompt version, tools used, and input data sources.
- Ensuring logs are tamper-evident, access-controlled, and retained for required periods.

These records support investigations, client dispute resolution, and regulatory exams. They also provide rich material for improving evaluation datasets.

Suitability, Best Execution, and Product Governance

Agents that influence investment decisions must respect policies such as suitability for clients, best execution, and product governance. Some practical patterns include:

Suitability-aware workflows.

For client-facing or advisory agents:

- Restrict access to client-level data to contexts where it is explicitly needed and permitted.
- Encode eligibility rules (e.g., professional vs. retail clients, jurisdictional restrictions) as machine-readable constraints.
- Require agents to call suitability-check tools before suggesting products or strategies, and block any recommendations that fail checks.

Best execution and routing policies.

For execution-support agents:

- Define which venues, order types, and algorithms are permissible for each asset class and client segment.
- Implement pre-trade checks that validate order parameters against best-execution policies.

- Log execution recommendations and outcomes so post-trade analysis can confirm that best-execution objectives are met over time.

Research independence and conflicts of interest.

Research-focused agents should respect firm policies on independence:

- Avoid mixing confidential order-flow data into research outputs unless explicitly allowed and ring-fenced.
- Tag and separate sell-side vs. buy-side content where relevant.
- Ensure prompts do not bias analysis toward house positions or inventory in ways that violate policy.

These constraints can be enforced by limiting the tools and data sources available to particular agent workflows and by inserting explicit policy checks before outputs are released.

Human-in-the-Loop Controls

In many contexts, regulations or firm policies demand that humans remain "in the loop." This does not mean agents are useless; it simply means they assist rather than replace regulated decision-makers.

Useful design patterns include:

- **Pre-approval queues**: agent-generated recommendations are queued for human review and sign-off, with clear UI highlighting key assumptions, constraints, and caveats.
- **Dual control for high-impact actions**: large trades, sensitive client communications, or deviations from standard policy require explicit approval by a second human, even if initiated by an agent.
- **Escalation triggers**: if the agent encounters ambiguous or high-risk situations (e.g., conflicting constraints, policy uncertainty), it must refuse to act and escalate to a designated human role.

These workflows should be codified and tested just as thoroughly as the agents themselves.

Security and Privacy Controls for Generative AI

Security and privacy risks are amplified when you connect powerful text models to sensitive financial data and live systems. Traditional controls (network segmentation, identity management, encryption) still apply, but LLMs introduce new attack surfaces and failure modes.

Access Control and Least Privilege

Apply the principle of least privilege at multiple layers:

- **User to agent**: who is allowed to invoke which agents, for which tasks, and with what scopes of data?
- **Agent to tools**: which workflows can call which tools (risk engines, OMSs, data sources), and with what parameter limits (e.g., maximum order size, allowed symbols)?
- **Agent to data**: what datasets and knowledge bases can the agent query, and under what masking or anonymization rules?

These policies can be enforced via:

- API gateways that check authorization and rate limits.
- Fine-grained entitlements on tools and data stores.
- Design-time constraints in the agent graph (e.g., some nodes simply do not have access to trading tools).

Data Minimization and Masking

To reduce the impact of any breach, expose only the minimum necessary data to LLMs:

- Prefer referencing client or trade IDs through opaque tokens rather than raw identifiers.

- Mask or tokenize sensitive fields (names, account numbers, exact positions) where possible.
- Use per-query filters so that agents only see data relevant to the current task and user.

When working with external LLM providers, ensure contractual and technical controls prevent training on your data unless explicitly intended and safe.

Defending Against Prompt Injection and Data Exfiltration

Prompt injection refers to attempts—often embedded in user inputs or external documents—to override the system's instructions or exfiltrate data. For example, a malicious email might contain hidden text instructing the agent to ignore risk limits or leak proprietary information.

Defenses include:

- **Input sanitization**: strip or neutralize suspicious markup, invisible characters, and obviously hostile instructions before they reach the core agent.
- **Separation of roles**: keep system and policy prompts distinct from user-provided content; do not allow user text to override core safety instructions.
- **Policy-checking layers**: use secondary models or rule-based filters to inspect proposed outputs for signs of data leakage, policy violations, or abnormal instructions before releasing them.
- **Tool-response validation**: treat outputs from tools and LLMs as untrusted and validate them against schemas, limits, and sanity checks before taking actions like placing trades.

Testing these defenses should be part of your red-teaming and stress-testing regimes, not just theoretical controls on paper.

Rate Limiting and Abuse Detection

Agents exposed to broader user bases (e.g., internal chatbots, client portals) should be protected against abuse and denial-of-service patterns:

- Implement per-user and per-desk rate limits on queries and tool calls.
- Monitor for abnormal patterns, such as scripted requests aiming to enumerate confidential information or exploit edge cases.
- Throttle or block access automatically when abusive patterns are detected, and alert security teams.

These measures protect both system stability and sensitive data.

Incident Response and Post-Mortems

Even with strong controls, incidents will occur: incorrect outputs, constraint breaches, security alerts, or near misses. The key is to respond quickly, limit damage, learn from the event, and feed improvements back into your evaluation and MLOps processes.

Incident Classification and Triage

First, define what constitutes an "incident" versus a minor issue. For LLM agents, classes might include:

- **Model error incidents**: incorrect or misleading outputs that reach users but do not cause direct financial loss or breach (e.g., an inaccurate research summary caught by an analyst).
- **Risk/compliance incidents**: outputs or actions that break limits, violate policies, or lead to regulatory concern (e.g., an unapproved product recommendation).
- **Security incidents**: suspected or confirmed data leaks, unauthorized access, or successful prompt injection attacks.

Each class has specific triage steps, owners, and escalation paths.

Immediate Containment Measures

When a serious incident is detected, containment may involve:

- Freezing or downgrading the model and/or agent workflow (e.g., switch to a safer baseline or advisory-only mode).

- Temporarily disabling certain tools or data sources (e.g., trading access) until the issue is understood.
- Narrowing access to affected agents to a smaller group of expert users.

Because you have versioned artifacts and deployment traceability from the MLOps setup, you can usually roll back to a previous safe configuration quickly.

Structured Post-Mortems and Feedback

After containment, conduct a post-mortem that focuses on learning rather than blame. Key questions include:

- What exactly happened? Reconstruct the sequence of inputs, model decisions, tool calls, and human interactions from logs.
- Which controls failed or were missing? Did evaluation suites miss this pattern? Were monitoring thresholds too loose? Was the workflow ambiguous?
- How do we prevent recurrence? This might involve:

- Adding new test cases and stress scenarios.
- Tightening prompts, constraints, or tool access.
- Adjusting SLOs and alerts.

Crucially, outcomes from post-mortems should be fed back into:

- The evaluation and backtesting frameworks (new edge cases and scenarios).
- The MLOps pipelines (additional automated checks or gating criteria).
- The model inventory and documentation (updated limitations and conditions of use).

Bringing It All Together

To make generative AI a durable part of your financial institution's capabilities rather than a fragile experiment, you must integrate it with existing risk, compliance, and security structures. The core practices discussed in this section can be summarized as follows:

- Treat LLMs, prompts, tools, and agent workflows as governed models, with clear inventory, ownership, and validation.
- Embed regulatory and policy requirements directly into workflows through constraints, tools, and human-in-the-loop controls.
- Implement strong security and privacy safeguards, with special attention to access control, data minimization, and prompt-injection defenses.
- Prepare for incidents with clear classification, containment, and post-mortem processes that loop back into evaluation and MLOps.

When these elements are in place, you can scale AI agents across research, trading, and client functions while maintaining the standards of safety, transparency, and accountability that regulators, clients, and internal stakeholders expect.

Chapter 6

Applications: Research Agents

In this chapter we stop treating models as clever calculators and start using them as tireless junior analysts. You will learn how to turn unstructured filings, transcripts, and news into clean, auditable facts; how to translate events and sentiment into leakage-controlled signals; and how to generate scenarios and reports that are both creative and tightly grounded in underlying data. The goal is not to replace your research process, but to surround it with agents that work at machine speed while preserving human-grade judgment and explainability.

6.1 Information Extraction from Financial Documents

In earlier chapters we treated large language models (LLMs) mostly as powerful calculators on text: you pass in a prompt, you get out an answer or a prediction. Research agents push this further. They must read the same raw material that human analysts read—10-K filings, earnings calls, investor presentations, regulatory notices, and news—

and distill it into structured, auditable facts that can drive quantitative research.

This section develops the document-centric layer of such agents. We will:

- survey the major financial document types and where useful information hides;
- design an end-to-end pipeline that turns messy documents into typed, queryable records;
- discuss layout awareness: tables, multi-column text, and page locations;
- show how to attach provenance (citations and spans) to every extracted fact;
- introduce basic evaluation and quality control.

The goal is to end up with something much more robust than "ask the model a question about this PDF." We want a system that can continuously ingest new documents, update a research knowledge base, and support downstream event and signal generation with clear audit trails.

From Documents to Research Facts

Analysts rarely care about documents for their own sake. They care about facts and relationships:

- **Entities**: companies, people, securities, regulators, products, geographies.
- **Events**: earnings releases, guidance changes, management turnover, lawsuits, covenant breaches, product launches, downgrades.
- **Attributes and numbers**: revenue by segment, margin trends, leverage ratios, share-count changes, notional sizes of facilities.

A good research agent therefore acts as a translator between:

$$\textit{unstructured, messy financial text and tables} \\ \rightarrow \\ \textit{structured, typed records keyed by time and instrument.}$$

Two properties are essential in finance:

Layout awareness The same number can appear in multiple places: main tables, footnotes, MD&A narrative, and exhibits. A naive OCR pass may scramble columns, lose table headers, or merge paragraphs. An effective agent must reason about the visual structure of the page: which cell belongs to which header, where a footnote applies, whether text is in a sidebar or the main flow.

Provenance Every extracted fact must be traceable: which document, page, table, and even character span did it come from? Without this, analysts and risk managers cannot trust the system, and compliance teams cannot review or audit it.

Before we design the architecture, we briefly review the main document types the agent must handle.

The Landscape of Financial Documents

Different documents contain different kinds of alpha-relevant information and present distinct technical challenges.

Regulatory filings (10-K, 10-Q, 20-F, etc.)

These are long, semi-structured documents. They include:

- primary financial statements (income, balance sheet, cash flow);
- detailed notes (revenue recognition, segment information, debt, contingencies);
- management discussion and analysis (MD&A);
- risk factors and legal proceedings;
- exhibits such as debt agreements or credit facility details.

Key difficulties:

- tables that span pages, with nested headers;
- cross-references (e.g., "see Note 7 to the consolidated financial statements");
- boilerplate interspersed with genuinely new disclosures;
- subtle wording changes year over year that can matter a lot.

Earnings call transcripts

These are mostly conversational text, structured by speaker:

- prepared remarks by executives;
- Q&A with sell-side analysts.

Challenges:

- imperfect transcripts (mis-heard proper names or numbers);
- nuanced sentiment, hedging, and forward-looking language;
- multiple events embedded in a single answer (e.g., guidance revisions plus commentary on competitive dynamics).

Investor presentations and decks

Slides often mix charts, bullet points, and small-font footnotes. Critical information such as non-GAAP reconciliation or covenant thresholds may appear in hard-to-read parts of the page. Layout extraction and OCR quality are central.

Broker research and news

Broker notes and news headlines capture external opinions and events. They may refer to multiple issuers, use tickers and aliases, and compress complex events into short text. Name resolution and careful event typing matter more than precise line-item numbers.

Across all of these, the agent needs a consistent internal view: a fact about "AAPL" should look the same whether it came from a 10-K, a CEO quote on an earnings call, or a newswire alert.

A Pipeline for Document-Centric Research Agents

At a high level, our research agent pipeline for information extraction has five stages:

1. **Ingestion and parsing**: get the document, normalize its format, and extract raw text and layout.
2. **Layout analysis**: reconstruct pages, blocks, tables, and reading order.
3. **LLM-based extraction**: map text and layout segments into structured schemas.
4. **Validation and post-processing**: check types, units, and relationships; attach confidence scores.
5. **Storage in a research knowledge base**: persist facts with metadata and provenance.

The following diagram summarizes this pipeline.

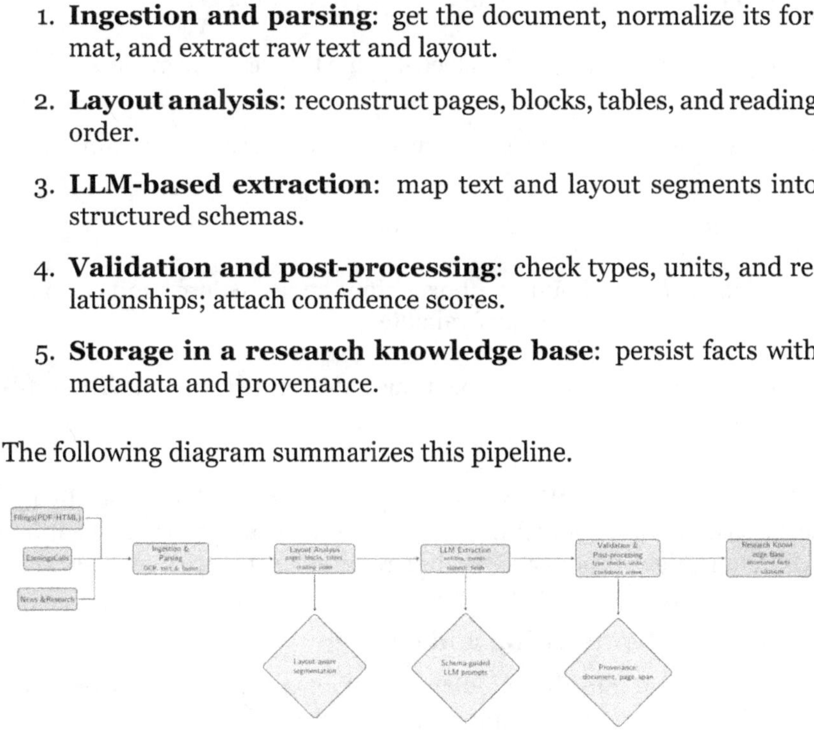

We now walk through each stage in more detail, emphasizing practical design choices.

Stage 1: Ingestion and Parsing

The ingestion layer is responsible for turning whatever you receive from a data vendor or website into a normalized, machine-readable form.

Format normalization

Documents may arrive as:

- PDFs (scanned or "born-digital");
- HTML pages (e.g., EDGAR filings, news websites);
- plain text or XML (news feeds, some transcript providers).

For each, you want a consistent internal representation containing:

- *raw text content* split by page or section;
- *layout hints*: bounding boxes, font styles, column indices, and table boundaries when available;
- *metadata*: document type, issuer, date/time, source, URL or filing ID.

When dealing with PDFs, high-quality OCR is essential, especially for scanned exhibits and old filings. For HTML, you must strip navigation, ads, and irrelevant boilerplate while retaining semantics such as table tags, headings, and list structures.

Document identification and keying

Every document must be uniquely identified and linked to one or more financial instruments. Common keys include:

- issuer identifiers (e.g., LEI, internal issuer ID);
- security identifiers (e.g., ISIN, CUSIP, or internal security ID);
- timestamps: as-of date (e.g., period end) and publication/availability time.

This keying is what later allows a downstream system to join extracted facts to prices, fundamental data, and positions.

Stage 2: Layout Analysis

Once you have normalized text and layout hints, the next step is to reconstruct how a human would read the document.

Why layout matters

Consider a revenue table with columns for regions and rows for years. A naive text extractor may output an interleaved stream of numbers. Without knowing which header applies to which number, you cannot reliably build a $(\text{year}, \text{region}) \rightarrow \text{revenue}$ table.

Similarly, a risk factor might be in a distinct section with its own heading and numbered list. Identifying this structure helps an LLM treat that section differently from, say, the auditor's report.

Typical layout elements

A layout-aware parser should at least distinguish:

- page boundaries;
- text blocks and paragraphs;
- headings and section titles;
- tables and their cells;
- footnotes, callouts, and sidebars;
- speaker turns in transcripts.

For PDFs, this usually involves clustering text boxes by coordinates and reading order. For HTML, you can leverage the DOM tree, tags (like <table>, <h1>-<h3>), and CSS classes.

Representing layout for the LLM

LLMs operate on sequences of tokens, not on rendered pages. You therefore need a textual representation that preserves enough layout information for the model to reason correctly. Common patterns include:

- **Structured markup**: wrap sections and tables in simple tags, e.g., <TABLE_START>...<TABLE_END>, <HEADER>, <CELL col=Region row=2024>.

- **Segmented inputs**: process each table or section separately with its own prompt, rather than the entire document at once.
- **Speaker labels**: prefix transcript lines with standardized speaker tags (e.g., SPEAKER: CEO, SPEAKER: Analyst).

The art is to provide enough structure that the model can align numbers and text with their roles, without overcomplicating the input.

Stage 3: LLM-Based Extraction

Now we come to the heart of the research agent: mapping text segments into structured, typed fields.

Designing schemas

Before writing any prompts, decide what you want the system to produce. Typical top-level schemas include:

- **Entity schema**: canonical name, identifiers, sector, country.
- **Event schema**: event type (e.g., earnings release, guidance change, management change, lawsuit), date/time, related entities, and key attributes.
- **Numeric schema**: metrics such as revenue, EBITDA, leverage, share count, each with value, unit, period, and any qualifiers (e.g., "adjusted", "non-GAAP").

For example, an EarningsGuidance event might have fields:

- fiscal_year: integer;
- metric: enumerated type (e.g., revenue, EPS);
- guidance_low, guidance_high: numbers;
- unit: string (e.g., "USD millions");
- is_update: boolean;

- source_section: string (e.g., "Prepared remarks", "Press release").

These schemas become your contract between the extraction layer and downstream systems.

Prompting with function calling or JSON output

Modern LLMs can be guided to emit structured outputs, such as JSON objects or function-call arguments. For each schema, you can design a prompt that:

1. explains the task in plain language;
2. provides a small number of examples (few-shot) to calibrate behavior;
3. specifies the expected JSON structure, field types, and any constraints;
4. includes the relevant text or table segment, clearly delimited.

For instance, you might pass in a single table of segment revenues, plus a short instruction: "Extract each business segment's revenue for the most recent fiscal year as numerical values in millions of USD."

The model's output is then parsed, validated, and stored in your knowledge base.

Hierarchical and multi-pass extraction

Long filings can exceed model context limits. Rather than trying to process an entire 10-K in one shot, use a hierarchical approach:

- **Pass 1: indexing**. Split the document into sections and ask the model to label which sections are relevant for which schema types (e.g., "Segment information appears in sections 3 and 5").
- **Pass 2: focused extraction**. For each relevant section or table, run a more detailed extraction prompt tailored to the schema.
- **Pass 3: cross-section reconciliation**. Combine results across sections, resolve conflicts or duplicates, and normalize units and periods.

For transcripts, you might first identify all answers that mention "guidance" and then extract a precise guidance object from those answers.

Stage 4: Validation, Uncertainty, and Human-in-the-Loop

LLMs are powerful, but fallible. In finance, a single digit error may have material consequences. We therefore wrap the model outputs in a set of deterministic checks and uncertainty handling strategies.

Type and range checks

Once you parse the model's JSON, you can enforce:

- *type constraints*: numbers must parse as floats or integers; dates must be valid calendar dates;
- *range constraints*: revenue cannot be negative; percentages should lie between 0 and 100 (or between 0 and 1 if normalized);
- *consistency*: totals should roughly equal the sum of components, within a tolerance.

If any of these fail, you can either discard the field, reduce its confidence score, or flag it for human review.

Cross-document consistency

For recurring data such as annual revenue, you will see multiple sources: the income statement, MD&A text, an investor deck, and external data vendors. Your agent can check:

- whether the extracted value matches trusted numerical feeds within a tolerance;
- whether an updated filing supersedes an earlier value (e.g., restatements);
- whether numbers trend plausibly over time (e.g., no 10x revenue jump unless explicitly labeled as an acquisition or restatement).

Discrepancies can be used to prioritize documents for manual review.

Confidence scores and abstention

Not every extraction should result in a stored fact. It is often better to say "I don't know" than to hallucinate. You can estimate confidence using:

- the model's own log probabilities or self-reported certainty (where available);
- agreement among multiple extraction prompts or models;
- pass/fail on the deterministic checks described above.

Based on this, you can set thresholds:

- above a high threshold: auto-accept into the knowledge base;
- between thresholds: store but flag as "needs review";
- below a low threshold: discard or keep only as a soft annotation.

This is where human-in-the-loop workflows fit naturally: analysts can correct or confirm extractions, and those corrections can be logged to improve future prompts and models.

Stage 5: Storing Facts with Full Provenance

The end product of the pipeline is not just values. It is values plus rich metadata:

- **What**: field name, value, unit, type.
- **Who/Which**: associated entities and instruments.
- **When**: event time, as-of time, and ingestion time.
- **Where**: source document ID, page number, section heading, table ID, and character span offsets.
- **How sure**: confidence score, validation flags.

A simple mental model is a set of tables in a research knowledge base, such as:

- Documents: one row per source document, with metadata and storage paths.
- Facts: one row per extracted fact, with foreign keys to Documents, entities, and instruments.
- Provenance: detailed references to page, section, and span for each fact.
- AuditLog: prompts, model versions, and human edits for traceability.

This structure enables powerful workflows:

- Analysts can click from a numeric signal in a backtest directly to the underlying disclosure that generated it.
- Compliance can review what the model "saw" and how it interpreted it when generating a report.
- Engineers can re-run extraction for a subset of documents with a new prompt or model and compare results on a regression test set.

Handling Difficult Cases: Tables, Footnotes, and Cross-References

Certain patterns repeatedly cause trouble and deserve special treatment.

Complex tables

Tables with multi-level headers, subtotal rows, or mixed units can confuse both parsers and LLMs. Practical tips include:

- preserving header hierarchies explicitly in the markup passed to the model (e.g., separate row-header and column-header labels);

- explicitly asking the model to ignore subtotal and total rows when extracting item-level values;
- segmenting very wide tables into smaller logical pieces (e.g., one per segment or region).

Footnotes and small print

Some of the most important caveats live in footnotes: non-GAAP definitions, one-off adjustments, and covenant definitions. To capture these:

- attach each footnote to the corresponding table cells or text spans at the layout stage;
- run specialized prompts on footnote text to extract flags (e.g., "one-time charge", "restatement", "change in methodology");
- connect those flags to the affected numeric fields in your knowledge base.

Cross-references and incorporation by reference

Filings frequently say "see Note X" or "as described in our Form 8-K filed on [date]." Handling this well requires:

- parsing cross-reference phrases and locating the target section or document;
- optionally bringing that referenced content into the extraction context when needed (e.g., when extracting covenant terms from a 10-K that points to an exhibit);
- linking facts in your knowledge base back to both the referencing and referenced documents.

This can be done incrementally: start with within-document references, then extend to cross-document ones as your system matures.

Evaluating an Extraction Agent

A research agent is only as useful as its accuracy and stability. Evaluation in this setting has a few layers.

Labeled test sets

You will need hand-labeled "gold" data for key schemas, drawn from a representative sample of documents. For each field, you can measure:

- **precision**: among extracted fields, what fraction are correct?
- **recall**: among true fields, what fraction did the system extract?

Because schemas are often multi-field objects (e.g., an event with ten attributes), you may want both field-level and object-level metrics (e.g., an event counts as correct only if all required fields match).

Regression tests across vintages

Issuers change their formatting and wording over time. To detect regressions:

- include multiple years and format variants of the same issuer in your test set;
- whenever you change prompts or models, re-run extraction on the test set and compare results;
- track metric time series to catch silent degradation.

Monitoring in production

Even with labeled data, most of your documents will be unlabeled. Useful online checks include:

- distributional checks (e.g., histograms of extracted leverage ratios, year-over-year growth rates);
- consistency checks across sources (filings vs. vendor feeds);
- alerting on unusual changes in extraction volume or failure rates.

These are early warning systems that something may have broken upstream (e.g., a data vendor changed its HTML templates) or downstream (e.g., a new model version interprets tables differently).

In this section we designed document-centric research agents that can read the main artifacts of public markets—filings, calls, news—and translate them into structured, auditable facts.

The key themes are:

- Treat documents as structured objects with layout, not just bags of words.
- Define clear schemas for entities, events, and numeric fields before writing prompts.
- Use LLMs as extraction engines within a disciplined pipeline: ingestion, layout analysis, schema-guided extraction, validation, and storage.
- Attach provenance and confidence to every fact; make abstention and human review part of the design.
- Evaluate systematically, both offline with labeled test sets and online with monitoring.

With this foundation in place, the next step is to turn these discrete, timestamped facts into time-aligned, leakage-controlled signals suitable for backtesting and portfolio integration, which we address in the following section.

6.2 Event and Sentiment-Driven Signal Generation

In the previous section we built document-centric agents that can read filings, earnings calls, and news, and convert them into structured, auditable facts. Those facts live in a research knowledge base as entities, events, and numeric attributes with clear provenance.

This section takes the next step: turning those extracted events and textual signals into *trading features* that can be backtested and, ultimately, integrated into portfolios.

Conceptually, we are moving:

from "What happened, according to the documents?"
to "How do we encode what happened as time-stamped, leakage-free variables that may predict returns or risk?"

To do this in a disciplined way, we will:

- define an event ontology and sentiment dimensions that sit on top of the extraction layer;
- show how to map raw extractions into timestamped, instrument-keyed events;
- discuss time alignment and leakage control, especially around earnings and calls;
- design practical event- and sentiment-based features;
- explain how to store these features in a research-ready feature store.

Throughout, we will keep two constraints in mind:

- Signals must be **well-defined and stable**: another researcher or regulator should be able to reconstruct them later.
- Signals must be **leakage-controlled**: they can only use information that was realistically available at the time.

From Extracted Facts to an Event Ontology

The extraction agent gives us low-level building blocks: discrete pieces of information such as:

- "Q2 2025 revenue guidance for Company X: 1.9–2.0 bn USD" (from a press release);

- "CFO resigns effective September 1" (from an 8-K or call transcript);
- "Regulator opens antitrust investigation" (from a newswire);
- sentences expressing optimism or concern in the CEO's prepared remarks.

To turn these into usable features, we need a consistent way of describing *what kind of thing* each fact is. This is the role of an **event ontology**.

Designing an event ontology

An event ontology is a catalog of event types and their attributes. You can think of it as a typed dictionary of "things that matter" for your investment process. Examples:

- **Earnings-related events**
- EarningsRelease: including realized EPS, revenue, surprise vs. consensus.
- GuidanceChange: including metric (EPS, revenue), direction (up, down, withdrawn), and magnitude.
- **Management and governance**
- ManagementChange: new or departing CEO/CFO, board changes.
- CompensationChange: major revisions to incentive plans.
- **Regulatory and legal**
- RegulatoryAction: investigations, fines, license changes.
- Litigation: material lawsuits filed or settled.
- **Business operations**
- ProductLaunch, PlantClosure, MajorContract, M&AAnnouncement.
- **ESG and incidents**

- EnvironmentalIncident, LaborDispute, DataBreach.

Each event type has:

- required fields (event time, issuer, description);
- type-specific fields (e.g., for GuidanceChange: old range, new range, metric, horizon);
- optional sentiment fields (e.g., tone of commentary surrounding the event).

Mapping extracted facts into events

The extraction agent may already output structured objects that closely resemble events. If not, you can add a light additional classification layer:

- Take an extracted fact (for example, a paragraph plus any associated numeric fields).
- Run an LLM classifier with a small set of examples to assign:
- an event type from the ontology (or "None");
- any missing attributes (e.g., direction of change inferred from wording).
- Store a canonical event record in your event store.

To remain stable over time, event definitions should be versioned. If you later refine the ontology (for instance, splitting GuidanceChange into "soft" vs. "hard" warnings), keep both the old and new definitions accessible and clearly labeled.

Sentiment as a Structured Signal

Events capture *what* happened. Sentiment captures *how it was framed.*

Textual sentiment in finance goes beyond simple "positive vs. negative." It is often multi-dimensional:

- **Tone**: broadly positive, neutral, or negative.
- **Conviction**: how strong or tentative the language is.
- **Uncertainty**: emphasis on risks, unknowns, or volatility.
- **Forward vs. backward-looking**: discussion of future outlook vs. past performance.

LLMs are well-suited to scoring text along such dimensions, especially when guided by clear rubrics and examples.

Defining sentiment dimensions

A practical sentiment schema for earnings calls might include:

- overall_tone: one of {very negative, negative, neutral, positive, very positive};
- forward_looking_tone: same five-point scale but focusing only on outlook statements;
- uncertainty_level: low/medium/high;
- surprise_alignment: whether management's tone is consistent with the numerical surprise (e.g., "numerically positive, but tone cautious").

Each of these categorical labels can later be mapped to numerical scores (e.g., -2 to +2) for use in models.

Attaching sentiment to spans and events

To avoid over-simplification, sentiment should be:

- *localized*: scored at the level of relevant sections, such as the CEO's prepared remarks, the CFO's comments, or the answers to specific questions.
- *linked*: attached to events in the ontology when appropriate. For example, a GuidanceChange event might carry a sentiment field summarizing how confidently the change was presented.

This linkage back to spans keeps sentiment grounded. In a backtest, you can always jump back from a surprising sentiment signal to the original language.

Time Alignment and Leakage Control

We now have timestamped events and associated sentiments. To use them as features, we must place them correctly on the trading timeline.

Two primary times matter:

- **Document time**: when something was said or published (e.g., the timestamp on a press release).
- **Availability time**: when that information was reasonably tradable in the market, after considering delays in dissemination, transcription, and processing.

Signals must be functions of information whose availability time is strictly before the returns they are intended to predict. Any violation here leads to look-ahead bias.

Earnings releases and calls

Earnings are a canonical example where timing is subtle:

- The *press release* may be published at 4:05pm, after the market close.
- The *call transcript* may become available 30–60 minutes later, or even the next morning, depending on your provider.

If you want to use:

- pure numerical surprise from the press release, you might assume it is available by the next trading day's open;
- nuanced sentiment from the call transcript, you may need to delay your feature further, for example, to the following day or a fixed number of hours after the scheduled call end.

The key is to adopt conventions that are:

- conservative enough to avoid implicit look-ahead;
- consistently applied across your universe and history;
- documented, so that later reviewers can understand your assumptions.

A timeline illustration

The following figure illustrates how an earnings release and call are transformed into leakage-controlled features.

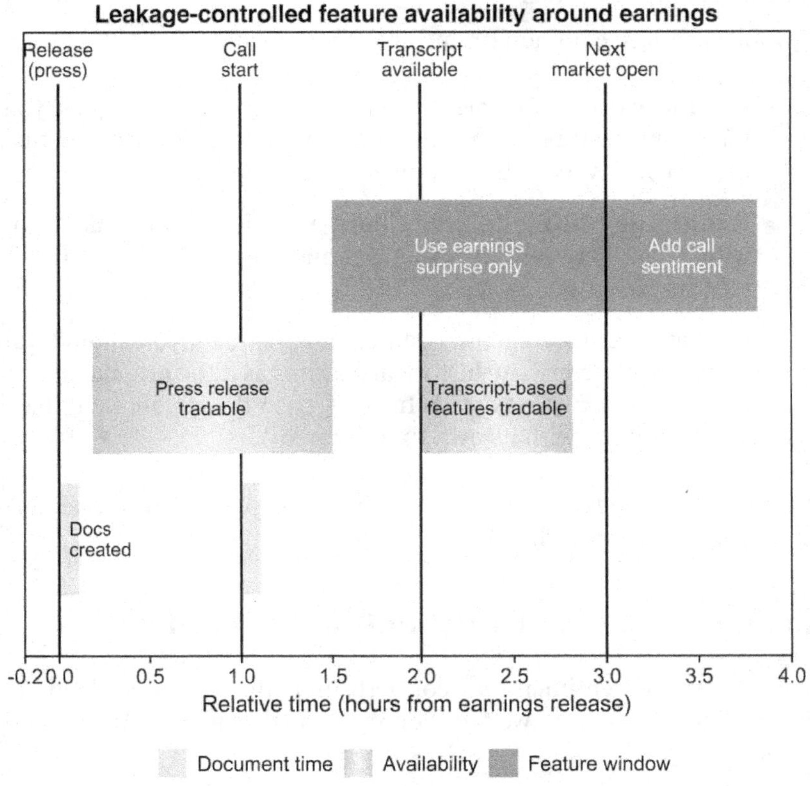

In this stylized example:

- earnings surprise features become usable after the press release has had time to reach the market and your systems (for example, from $t = 1.5$ onward);
- call-based sentiment features become usable only after the transcript is processed (from $t = 3$ onward), and therefore can only influence returns from that point.

In backtesting, you would align your predictors accordingly, making sure that any return window you try to predict starts *after* feature availability.

Other timing nuances

Beyond earnings, common timing challenges include:

- **Intraday news**: For high-frequency or intraday strategies, you may align features at minute-level or finer granularity, taking into account vendor timestamps and processing delays.
- **Regulatory filings**: Some filings are released after hours or with delays between the formal submission time and when your feed receives them.
- **Restatements**: When a restatement is issued, you should not retroactively overwrite historical features as if the original, incorrect numbers never existed. Instead, treat the restatement itself as a new event with its own timestamp.

A conservative rule of thumb is: when in doubt, push feature availability later rather than earlier.

Engineering Event and Sentiment Features

Once events and sentiments are correctly time-aligned, we can begin to engineer features. Here we focus on patterns that make intuitive and economic sense.

Signed sentiment scores

A basic building block is a signed sentiment score $s_{i,t}$ for instrument i at time t, derived from one or more texts. Practical variations include:

- **Single-source scores**: e.g., overall tone of the most recent earnings call.
- **Aggregated scores**: weighted averages of sentiment across multiple news headlines in a day, perhaps with higher weights for more reputable sources or more detailed articles.
- **Segmented scores**: separate sentiment for management commentary vs. external analysts or journalists.

These scores can be used directly or transformed (for example, clipped to a range, z-scored across the cross-section, or smoothed over time).

Event intensity and recency

Events are often most informative when they are:

- recent;
- rare (e.g., first investigation in several years);
- clustered (e.g., multiple downgrades in a week).

Feature patterns that capture this include:

- **Count features**: number of events of a given type in the past K days (e.g., three negative news headlines about lawsuits in the last week).
- **Time-since-last-event**: days since the last GuidanceChange or RegulatoryAction.
- **Decay-weighted intensity**: assign each event a weight that decays with age (for example, exponentially) and sum over a lookback window.

Because your events are stored as discrete, timestamped records keyed by instrument, computing these features is straightforward once you have chosen your lookback horizons.

Discrete labels for complex situations

Some situations are too nuanced for a single numerical score. For example, distinguishing between:

- a "soft" guidance cut, where management lowers the range slightly but emphasizes one-off headwinds and future opportunity;
- a "hard" warning, where management signals structural challenges and sustained margin pressure.

Here, you can use LLMs as *labelers*:

- Define a set of scenario labels (e.g., {soft cut, hard warning, reaffirmation, upgrade}).
- Provide the model with a detailed rubric and several examples of each label.
- For each relevant event (e.g., any change in guidance), ask the model to assign a label.

These labels then become categorical features that can be encoded using dummy variables or embeddings in your models.

Interactions with cross-sectional features

Event and sentiment features often gain power when combined with other characteristics:

- **Size**: a negative event may have larger price impact for smaller, less liquid stocks.
- **Valuation**: the same positive news can be interpreted differently depending on starting valuation.
- **Volatility**: sentiment surprises may matter more when volatility is elevated.

You can create interaction features such as:

- sentiment score × size decile;
- event count in past week × prior 1-month volatility.

These combinations should be interpretable and economically motivated, not purely mechanical.

Building a Research-Ready Feature Store

As your library of event and sentiment features grows, organization becomes critical. A **feature store** is a structured repository that standardizes how features are defined, computed, versioned, and served.

Core requirements

A research-ready feature store for event and sentiment signals should provide:

- **Clear definitions**: each feature has a human-readable description, mathematical or algorithmic definition, and references to the underlying event/sentiment schemas.
- **Stable joins**: features are indexed by instrument and time in a way that can be reliably joined to price and fundamental data.
- **Versioning**: changes to feature definitions, model prompts, or extraction pipelines result in new feature versions, with old versions retained for reproducibility.
- **Backfill logic**: careful handling of how features are backfilled historically, respecting the same availability-time conventions as in real-time.

Preventing common biases

Well-designed infrastructure also helps prevent classic research pitfalls:

- **Look-ahead bias**: enforced by construction if every feature has an explicit availability timestamp and joins only allow using features strictly prior to the return window.

- **Survivorship bias**: avoided by basing your instrument universe and identifiers on time-varying membership, including delisted or acquired names.
- **Re-simulation bias**: controlled by freezing older feature versions; backtests conducted today should be reproducible later even if the extraction models improve.

In practice, this often means:

- representing features in a time-partitioned storage format;
- maintaining metadata that ties each feature value back to:
- the event(s) that contributed to it;
- the underlying documents;
- the model and prompt versions that produced the event and sentiment labels.

In this section we have taken the structured, provenance-rich outputs of document research agents and shown how to transform them into usable trading features:

- We introduced an *event ontology* to organize extracted facts into economically meaningful types.
- We showed how to define multi-dimensional *sentiment* that goes beyond simple positivity scores and is grounded in specific text spans.
- We emphasized *time alignment and leakage control*, especially around earnings releases and calls, and illustrated how feature availability must lag document and processing times.
- We presented practical patterns for *event and sentiment feature engineering*: signed scores, intensity, recency, and interaction with cross-sectional characteristics.
- We motivated the need for a *research-ready feature store* that enforces consistent definitions, versioning, and bias control.

With these building blocks, research teams can move from raw narrative content to well-defined, testable signals. In the next section, we will focus on the "last mile": using these signals, together with structured data, to generate grounded scenarios and automated reports that humans can trust and regulators can audit.

6.3 Scenario Generation and Report Automation

In the first section of this chapter, we built document-centric research agents that can read real-world financial documents and emit structured, auditable facts. In the second, we transformed those facts into time-aligned, leakage-controlled signals suitable for backtesting and portfolio integration.

This section focuses on the "last mile" of the research process: turning those data and signals into scenarios, narratives, and reports that humans can read, challenge, and act on. Here, generative AI becomes most visible to front-office users, but it must remain firmly grounded in the underlying data and subject to rigorous controls.

Our objectives are:

- to distinguish unconstrained storytelling from *grounded* generation in finance;
- to show how agents can use the research knowledge base and feature store to generate base, bull, bear, and stress scenarios;
- to describe patterns for automating research reports while preserving analyst judgment and compliance oversight;
- to introduce guardrails and provenance mechanisms that keep generative outputs auditable and defensible.

From Facts and Signals to Grounded Narratives

It is tempting to treat an LLM as an all-purpose author: "Write me a report on Company X." In finance, this is dangerous. A model that freely invents numbers, events, or causal stories undermines trust and introduces unquantified risk.

Instead, we want **grounded generative systems**: agents that can write, but only by:

- querying approved data sources (the knowledge base and feature store);
- staying within explicit rules about what may or may not be said;
- justifying each important claim with traceable evidence.

A simple mental picture is:

facts and signals $\rightarrow$ *structured outline* $\rightarrow$ *draft narrative* $\rightarrow$ *reviewed and approved report.*

The agent participates in each step, but data and humans remain in control.

Scenario Generation: Structuring Uncertainty

Investment decisions are almost always about the future under uncertainty: revenues might grow or shrink; margins might compress; regulation may tighten or loosen. Analysts handle this by reasoning in terms of *scenarios*.

A **scenario** is a coherent story about how key variables could evolve, usually with:

- a label (e.g., base, bull, bear, stress);
- assumptions about drivers (e.g., demand growth, pricing, cost inflation, FX, regulation);
- consequences for financials (revenue, margins, leverage);
- narrative explanation: "why" this path might occur.

Generative agents help by systematizing and documenting this process, not by replacing human judgment.

Ingredients for scenarios

A grounded scenario engine typically draws on four kinds of inputs:

- **Current state**: latest financials, guidance, balance sheet metrics, and operational KPIs from the knowledge base.
- **Historical patterns**: past cycles, similar events in the same company or peers, and how outcomes unfolded.
- **Signals**: event- and sentiment-based features that may indicate risk or opportunity (e.g., repeated negative guidance surprises, rising regulatory event counts).
- **Exogenous assumptions**: user-specified macro or thematic views (e.g., "rates stay higher for longer", "commodity prices fall 20%"), or outputs from separate models.
- **Model outputs**: projections from forecasting models or risk systems, with confidence intervals or stress responses.

The agent's task is to combine these pieces into internally consistent scenario narratives and, where appropriate, structured forecasts.

A simple scenario template

For many use cases, a relatively simple, repeatable scenario template is sufficient. For example, for each covered company:

- **Base case**: "What is most likely given current guidance, consensus, and our signals?" Use extrapolations and modest deviations from guidance where justified.
- **Bull case**: "What upside is plausible if things go better than expected?" Tie to favorable drivers such as faster demand, stronger pricing, or margin expansion.
- **Bear case**: "What downside is plausible if identified risks materialize?" Connect to specific risk factors, negative sentiment, or adverse events.

- **Stress case**: "What happens under a severe but coherent shock?" For example, a deep recession or regulatory clampdown.

The agent can populate each case with:

- numerical paths (e.g., revenue, EBIT margin, leverage) derived from models or rule-based sensitivities;
- bullet-point assumptions (e.g., "ASP falls 5% per year in bear case");
- short textual explanations explicitly referencing data and risk factors.

Using the knowledge base and feature store

To stay grounded, the agent should never guess. Instead, it issues explicit queries such as:

- "Retrieve last eight quarters of revenue and EBIT margin for issuer A."
- "Fetch last five GuidanceChange events and their directions."
- "Get average and worst historical drawdowns during past downturns for this industry."
- "Retrieve event-based features signaling regulatory risk (counts, intensities)."

The responses from these queries become the raw material for scenarios. The agent can then:

- compute simple transformations (growth rates, margins, leverage ratios);
- apply scenario rules (e.g., apply a specified shock to volumes or prices);
- ask the LLM to verbalize the implications: "Given these inputs, describe a plausible path for revenue and margins in the bear case, referencing the key risks that drive it."

Because the inputs are structured, you can log exactly which data points and signals influenced each scenario.

Counterfactuals and "what-if" questions

Analysts and risk managers often ask counterfactual questions like:

- "What if rates remain 200 bps higher for three years?"
- "What if the new product launch is delayed by one year?"

Here, the generative agent acts as an orchestrator:

- interpret the user's question and map it to changes in assumptions (e.g., cost of debt, demand growth, timing of cash flows);
- propagate those changes through sensitivity models or simple heuristics (e.g., how interest expense changes, how revenue paths shift);
- generate a short scenario narrative explaining the consequences, emphasizing which variables are most affected and how sensitive the overall thesis is.

Importantly, the agent should keep a clear boundary between:

- **assumptions** (stated explicitly, possibly user-provided);
- **mechanical implications** (results of models or rules);
- **interpretive commentary** (how an analyst might think about risk/reward).

This separation makes the process transparent and reviewable.

Report Automation: Templates, Roles, and Workflows

Once we can generate grounded scenarios, the next step is to package them into reports: company notes, sector reviews, macro decks, and portfolio risk summaries. Automating parts of this work can save considerable time, but only if done with clear structure.

Thinking in templates

A **report template** separates content (what is being said) from presentation (how it looks) and from constraints (what must or must not be said). Typical sections of a company report might include:

- Investment summary and rating;
- Business overview and recent developments;
- Key drivers and risks;
- Scenario analysis (base/bull/bear/stress);
- Valuation and expected return;
- ESG and other qualitative considerations;
- Disclosures and compliance language.

For each section, we can specify:

- its purpose (e.g., "succinctly explain the investment thesis and main catalysts");
- what data it should draw from (e.g., scenarios, event history, sentiment indicators, valuation metrics);
- stylistic constraints (e.g., concise bullet points vs. full paragraphs; no speculative language beyond a certain threshold).

The agent's role is to fill these templates using queries to the knowledge base and feature store, plus controlled generation.

Roles: data retriever, drafter, and companion editor

Conceptually, we can assign three roles to the agent:

1. Data retriever

The agent first gathers the relevant inputs:

- current valuation metrics (multiples, target vs. current price);
- recent events (earnings, guidance updates, management changes);
- sentiment summaries (e.g., call tone, news polarity);
- scenario outputs (numerical projections and assumptions).

This step is retrieval and transformation only; no narrative yet.

2. Drafting assistant

Given structured inputs and a section-specific prompt, the LLM produces text such as:

- a one-paragraph investment summary;
- a bullet list of top three risks, each tied to an underlying event or factor;
- a concise explanation of differences between base and bear cases.

Each draft is accompanied by metadata: which data points were used, and pointers back to the underlying facts and signals.

3. Companion editor

Human analysts or risk managers should remain in the loop. The agent can:

- propose alternative phrasings for clarity or brevity;
- highlight inconsistencies between narrative and data (e.g., if the text claims "low leverage" but metrics show high leverage);
- check that required disclosures and constraints are satisfied.

The final approval always lies with a human or with a separate approval workflow endorsed by compliance.

Guardrails, Compliance, and Provenance

Generative systems in finance must operate under tight guardrails. At a minimum, these guardrails should address:

- factual consistency with the data layer;
- regulatory and internal policy constraints;
- traceability of how outputs were produced.

Factual consistency checks

Before any generated report section is accepted, an automated checker can:

- re-parse the generated text and extract key numeric statements (e.g., growth rates, margins, leverage);
- compare these to the values in the feature store for the same date and issuer;
- flag discrepancies beyond a tolerance, or force the agent to revise the text.

This creates a feedback loop: if text says "mid-single-digit revenue growth" but the data show 12%, the check fails and the agent must either correct the statement or adjust the language (for example, "low double-digit" instead of "mid-single-digit").

Policy and compliance rules

Compliance constraints may include:

- prohibition on certain phrases (e.g., guaranteeing returns);
- requirements to state risks alongside recommendations;
- restrictions on coverage or commentary under blackout policies.

You can embed these as machine-readable rules that the agent must respect:

- pre-generation: shaping prompts to avoid disallowed content;
- post-generation: scanning output for forbidden terms or missing disclosures, and either blocking or requesting revision.

Where rules are complex, a specialized "compliance checker" model, itself constrained and audited, can assist.

Audit logs and provenance

For each generated report, the system should maintain an audit trail including:

- which data sources were queried (knowledge base tables, feature sets);
- which prompts were used (including versions and templates);
- which model versions were called;
- all intermediate drafts and human edits;
- the final approved text and associated metadata (e.g., timestamp, approver).

At the level of individual claims in the text, we can maintain **provenance tags**: structured links back to:

- the specific fact or feature in the data layer (e.g., revenue growth for FY2024);
- the original documents or events that underlie that fact (e.g., the 10-K page and section that disclosed it).

This provenance serves three purposes:

- transparency: readers, reviewers, and regulators can see what evidence supports a statement.
- error correction: if an input fact is later corrected (for example, due to a restatement), downstream narratives can be identified and updated.

- model improvement: logged disagreements between humans and the agent can be used as training data to refine prompts and behavior.

Deployment Patterns and Success Metrics

Finally, we consider how scenario and reporting agents are deployed in practice, and how to measure whether they are helping rather than hindering.

Interaction modes

Common deployment patterns include:

- **Interactive copilot**: embedded in the analyst's research environment, the agent can answer questions ("Summarize key risks for Company X") and draft report sections on demand.
- **Periodic automation**: scheduled jobs generate recurring artifacts such as weekly sector dashboards, portfolio risk summaries, or monthly scenario reviews.
- **Event-driven updates**: when a significant event occurs (e.g., earnings release, regulatory action), the agent prepares a quick-turnaround note highlighting changes to the thesis or scenarios.

Each pattern should integrate naturally with approval workflows, version control, and document management systems.

Measuring success

Beyond technical validation, you should track practical success metrics such as:

- **Time saved**: reduction in analyst hours spent on mechanical drafting and updating of standard sections.
- **Error rates**: frequency of factual or compliance errors before and after introducing the agent.
- **Coverage consistency**: how uniform scenario structures and risk discussions are across a large coverage universe.

- **User adoption and satisfaction**: whether analysts actually use and trust the tools, and in which tasks (drafting, checking, brainstorming).

These feedback loops help refine not only the models and prompts but also the surrounding process: which parts of reporting should be automated, which should remain firmly manual, and where hybrid approaches work best.

This section has described how to move from structured facts and signals to grounded, auditable narratives:

- We distinguished unconstrained text generation from *grounded* generation, where all important claims trace back to vetted data.
- We showed how to construct base, bull, bear, and stress scenarios by combining current state, historical patterns, signals, and explicit assumptions.
- We outlined report automation patterns based on templates, with the agent acting as data retriever, drafting assistant, and companion editor under human oversight.
- We emphasized guardrails: factual consistency checks, policy rules, and detailed provenance and audit logs.
- We discussed deployment patterns and success metrics that matter in production research settings.

Together with the previous sections on extraction and signal generation, this completes the core picture of research agents: systems that read the same documents humans do, organize their content into structured, time-aware signals, and then help transform those signals into scenarios and reports that are faster to produce, easier to audit, and more consistent across an investment organization.

Chapter 7

Applications: Trading Agents

This chapter moves from backtests to the trading floor. We take the signals, models, and tools developed earlier and wire them into full-stack trading agents that can design portfolios, execute intelligently in fragmented markets, and adapt as regimes shift. The goal is not just to trade, but to build agents that understand risk, respect microstructure, and keep learning-without blowing up when reality disagrees with the research notebook.

7.1 Strategy Design and Portfolio Construction

In the previous chapters we treated trading agents mainly as information-processing systems: they ingest data, generate predictions or alpha signals, and learn patterns from markets. In practice, however, an agent is judged not by the quality of its forecasts alone, but by the portfolios and trades that result. A collection of promising alphas is only the beginning. To become investable, those signals must be transformed into coherent, risk-aware positions that respect constraints, costs, and the realities of execution.

This section explains that transformation. We start from a realistic picture of what "alphas" look like inside a generative-AI-enabled research stack. We then show how a strategy layer turns those alphas into expected-return views, integrates a risk model, and constructs portfolios using optimization and simpler score-based rules. Throughout, we highlight where generative AI agents fit: not as opaque black boxes that magically output positions, but as orchestration and analysis tools wrapped around a transparent numerical core.

From Alphas to an Investable Strategy

Inside a modern trading system, alphas are diverse and messy. Different research workflows, including those assisted by generative AI, may produce:

- **Statistical signals**: e.g., a mean-reversion score on equities, a carry signal in FX, or a volatility forecast for options.
- **Fundamental and textual signals**: e.g., sentiment extracted from earnings calls, structured outputs from LLMs that summarize news risk, or changes in analyst tone.
- **Execution-level signals**: e.g., short-horizon order book imbalance, flow toxicity measures, or predicted short-term impact.

Each of these comes with its own scale, horizon, and reliability. The role of the strategy design layer is to:

- **Standardize** signals so that they can be compared.
- **Combine** them into a unified expected-return view per asset.
- **align*** those views with a risk model and investment objective.
- **Produce** target positions and a trade list that downstream execution agents can handle.

A helpful way to think about this is as a pipeline:

$$\text{signals} \rightarrow \text{expected returns} \rightarrow \text{risk model \& constraints} \rightarrow \text{portfolio} \rightarrow \text{trade list}$$

An LLM- or generative-AI-based agent may assist at every stage — by cleaning metadata, diagnosing conflicts between signals, suggesting constraint sets, or generating stress scenarios — but the actual mapping from inputs to portfolio should be explicit, auditable, and as simple as the problem allows.

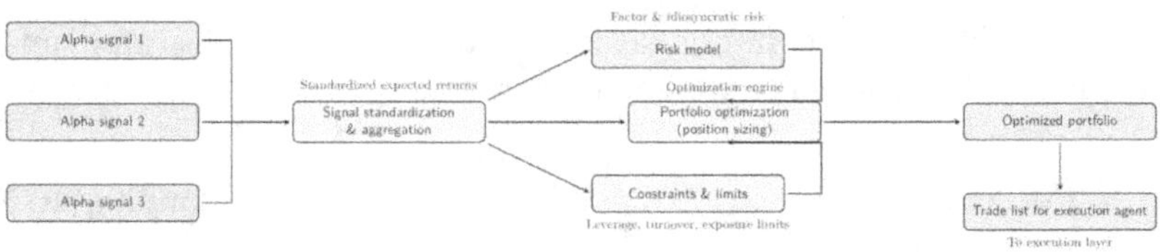

Standardizing and Combining Alpha Signals

Before any optimization, we need a consistent representation of "view" across assets. This often means mapping heterogeneous signals into a common scale of expected returns or scores.

Basic standardization

Common steps include:

- **De-meaning and scaling**: For each signal, subtract the cross-sectional mean and divide by its cross-sectional standard deviation. This produces a "z-score" that expresses how extreme a value is relative to its peers.
- **Direction alignment**: Ensure all signals are aligned so that higher values always mean "more attractive" (e.g., higher expected return, lower risk).

- **Robust clipping**: Limit extreme z-scores to a reasonable range (e.g., between -3 and $+3$) to avoid a single noisy observation dominating the portfolio.

Generative AI agents can assist here by managing metadata: tracking which signals are inverted, which are long-horizon vs. intraday, and suggesting reasonable clipping thresholds based on diagnostic plots they generate and summarize.

Signal combination into expected returns

Once signals share a common scale, we combine them. A simple and transparent approach is a weighted average:

- **Fixed weights**: e.g., 50% slow value signal, 30% quality, 20% sentiment.
- **Performance-based weights**: adjust weights over time based on rolling out-of-sample performance of each signal.
- **Contextual weights**: e.g., tilt more heavily toward defensive signals in stressed regimes; an LLM-driven agent might detect regime changes from news flow and suggest weight shifts within pre-defined bounds.

The result is a single expected-return score for each asset (or a small set of scores corresponding to different horizons). At this stage the strategy agent has a view, but not yet a position. To size positions responsibly, we need to understand risk.

Integrating a Risk Model

A risk model translates positions into risk. It answers questions like: "If I hold these weights, how volatile is my portfolio, what factors drive that volatility, and how correlated are my holdings?"

For our purposes, the key ideas are:

- **Factor structure**: Exposures to systematic drivers (e.g., market, sector, value, momentum) plus idiosyncratic risk.
- **Covariance**: A matrix that encodes how assets move together.
- **Risk attribution**: Decomposing total portfolio variance by asset, factor, and strategy component.

A trading agent does not need to derive these from scratch. It needs to be able to:

- Query the risk model for candidate portfolios.
- Enforce that the final portfolio respects risk budgets (e.g., not more than a certain volatility or a certain exposure to the market factor).
- Explain, in human-readable language, why a given portfolio has the risk profile it does.

Generative AI is particularly useful for the third task: taking numerical risk reports and converting them into concise natural-language narratives that portfolio managers and risk officers can assess.

Constraints: Encoding the Investment Mandate

Real portfolios live under a web of constraints. These protect investors, ensure regulatory compliance, and align with the strategy's mandate. Some common categories:

- **Capital and leverage**: Total gross and net exposure limits; maximum leverage ratios.
- **Position bounds**: Minimum and maximum weight per asset, sector, or region; caps on short exposure.
- **Turnover and trading**: Limits on how much of the portfolio can change per day; maximum participation rates in daily volume.

- **Factor and style exposure**: Bounds on exposure to market beta, sectors, or style factors (value, momentum, size, etc.).
- **Liquidity & concentration**: Minimum average daily volume thresholds; constraints to avoid overly concentrated portfolios.

An important design principle for trading agents is **constraint transparency**. Constraints should be:

- **Declarative**: Represented as a set of explicit rules or inequalities that can be inspected.
- **Centralized**: Managed in a configuration store that strategy agents, risk systems, and execution agents all read from.
- **Versioned**: Changes are logged with timestamps, rationale, and approvals, enabling audit and rollback.

Generative AI can assist in drafting constraint sets from high-level mandates. For example, given a textual investment policy, an LLM-based tool can propose a machine-readable constraint schema, which human experts then review and approve.

Portfolio Construction Techniques

We now have three essential components:

- Expected returns per asset (from combined alphas).
- A risk model that maps weights to risk.
- A set of constraints that encode our mandate and practical limits.

Portfolio construction is the process of mapping these into target weights. We will highlight two broad families: simple score-based methods and optimization-based methods.

Score-based ranking and bucketing

A useful starting point, especially for beginners, is to avoid optimization altogether and use score-based rules. For example:

- **Rank-and-hold**: Rank assets by expected return. Go long the top decile and short the bottom decile, subject to liquidity and concentration constraints.
- **Equal-weighted buckets**: Assign equal weights to all assets in a bucket, scaling so that total long and short exposure meets a target.
- **Volatility or risk-parity scaling**: Adjust each asset's weight based on its historical volatility, so that each position contributes similar risk.

These rules are simple, transparent, and often surprisingly effective. They also make it easy for a generative-AI research agent to simulate "what if" variations: different bucket sizes, rebalancing frequencies, or volatility scaling schemes.

However, score-based methods can struggle to incorporate many constraints and a rich risk model simultaneously. For that we turn to optimization.

Mean-variance style optimization

A classical approach, still very relevant in practice, is to choose weights that balance expected return against risk as measured by the covariance matrix. Conceptually:

- We want more weight in assets with higher expected returns, *all else equal.*
- We want less weight in assets that increase portfolio risk too much, especially if they are highly correlated with existing positions.
- We must satisfy all constraints (bounds, factor exposures, leverage, turnover, etc.).

This leads to a numerical optimization problem. The details can be complex, but the intuition is simple: search over all portfolios that satisfy the rules and pick the one that maximizes a risk-adjusted objective.

In practice, a trading agent should:

- Use a well-tested, deterministic optimization library.
- Expose key knobs (risk aversion, transaction cost penalties, etc.) as configuration parameters rather than hard-coded values.
- Log inputs and outputs for every optimization run, enabling replay and forensic analysis.

Generative AI can operate around this engine: proposing candidate parameter settings, explaining sensitivity analyses, or summarizing how the optimal portfolio would change under alternative constraints.

Risk-parity and other robust formulations

For some strategies, especially those focused on diversification rather than pure alpha, the objective is framed in terms of equalizing or controlling contributions to risk. Examples include:

- **Risk parity**: Choose weights so that each asset or asset class contributes roughly the same amount to total portfolio volatility.
- **Maximum diversification**: Maximize a measure of diversification subject to return and risk constraints.
- **Robust or worst-case optimization**: Incorporate uncertainty in the risk or return estimates, seeking portfolios that perform reasonably well across plausible parameter variations.

These approaches are especially attractive when expected returns are noisy or hard to estimate — precisely the situation that often arises with complex, high-dimensional alphas produced by AI models. An LLM-based assistant can help diagnose when expected-return estimates are unstable and suggest shifting weight toward more robust formulations.

Accounting for Costs, Turnover, and Market Impact

A portfolio that looks attractive on paper may be impossible or unwise to trade. Three frictions are particularly important:

- **Transaction costs**: Fees, commissions, and bid-ask spreads.
- **Slippage**: The difference between theoretical prices and actual execution prices.
- **Market impact**: The price moves caused by your own trading, especially at large size or in illiquid names.

To address these, strategy design must explicitly penalize trading in the construction step, not only at the execution layer. Common techniques include:

- **Turnover penalties**: Add a cost proportional to how much the portfolio changes from one period to the next, encouraging stability.
- **Volume-based limits**: Cap trade size as a fraction of average daily volume; these can be both constraints (hard limits) and cost components (larger trades incur higher modeled impact).
- **Nonlinear impact models**: Approximate costs that increase more than linearly with trade size, discouraging excessively large orders.

Generative AI agents can help here by:

- Extracting and updating liquidity statistics from market data feeds or broker reports.
- Generating natural-language explanations of how much performance is being sacrificed to reduce turnover.
- Proposing scenario analyses (e.g., "What if average spreads doubled?") and organizing the resulting simulations.

The key design principle is **capacity awareness**: your strategy should be sized and constructed with realistic assumptions about what execution agents can achieve, not what a frictionless backtest suggests.

From Target Portfolio to Trade List

Once the strategy layer has computed an optimal or otherwise chosen portfolio, it must express that decision as a trade list suitable for the execution layer. This involves:

- **Comparing** the new target weights with current holdings.
- **Translating** weight differences into quantities (shares, contracts, notional amounts).
- **Applying** per-name and portfolio-level trading limits (e.g., maximum daily turnover, volume participation caps).
- **Tagging** trades with metadata: strategy ID, priority, urgency, and any execution preferences.

A well-designed trading agent will:

- Perform basic sanity checks (e.g., no NaN positions, no gross or net exposures beyond allowed ranges) before emitting a trade list.
- Emit both a machine-readable format (for the execution engine) and a human-readable summary (for portfolio managers and risk teams).
- Log every trade recommendation together with the inputs (alphas, constraints, risk model snapshot) that generated it.

Generative AI is particularly helpful in assembling the human-readable view: it can cluster trades by theme ("adding to quality names in healthcare," "reducing cyclical exposure in emerging markets"), highlight the largest risk changes, and flag any trades that are near constraint boundaries.

The Role of Generative AI in Strategy Design

Throughout this section, we have treated generative AI not as the optimizer itself, but as an orchestration and explanation layer around a transparent portfolio-construction engine. This separation of concerns is crucial for risk, compliance, and operational reliability.

Concretely, LLM-based agents can:

- **Manage configuration**: Keep constraints, parameter settings, and strategy variants organized and versioned, providing natural-language interfaces to inspect and modify them under human supervision.

- **Assist research**: Propose new combinations of signals, generate stress scenarios, and summarize backtest results, while leaving the actual numerical evaluation to deterministic code.

- **Explain behavior**: Convert risk reports, optimization diagnostics, and trade lists into narratives that human stakeholders can critique.

- **Monitor and alert**: Watch for unusual portfolio changes, constraint boundary hits, or drifts in risk profile, and surface them quickly.

Meanwhile, the **core** mapping from alphas and risk to positions should remain stable, testable, and subject to traditional validation and backtesting. In the next section, when we descend into the execution layer and market microstructure, we will see how similar principles apply: generative AI can suggest, analyze, and explain, but deterministic components retain control over order placement and risk limits.

By structuring strategy design and portfolio construction in this way, we allow trading agents to benefit from the flexibility and creativity of generative models without sacrificing the rigor, transparency, and safety required in professional finance.

7.2 Execution Agents and Market Microstructure

In the previous section we stopped at the point where the strategy layer has produced a target portfolio and a corresponding trade list. That is a statement of *intent*: which instruments to buy or sell, and in what size. Markets, however, only respond to *orders*. The role of the execution agent is to translate portfolio intent into concrete orders, send those orders to appropriate venues, and manage the trade-off between cost, risk, and information leakage under strict safety controls.

This section moves from the relatively slow world of portfolio construction to the fast, microstructural world of order books, queues, and latency. We first review the basic building blocks of modern market microstructure. Then we introduce an architecture for execution agents that takes batched trade lists from the strategy layer and decomposes them into execution schedules and child orders. We emphasize how agents navigate fragmented liquidity and manage market impact, and how risk and compliance guardrails are embedded directly into the execution loop. Throughout, generative AI components play a supporting role: monitoring, explaining anomalies, and assisting parameter selection, while deterministic logic retains final authority over when and how orders are placed.

A Brief Tour of Market Microstructure

To understand execution agents, we need a concrete picture of the environment they operate in. At a high level, most electronic markets today are organized around a *limit order book*:

- **Limit orders** specify a price and quantity: “Buy 1,000 shares at $99 or better.” They rest in the book until matched or canceled.
- **Market orders** specify quantity only: “Buy 1,000 shares now.” They execute immediately against the best available prices in the book, often paying the bid-ask spread.
- **Bid and ask**: The highest buy price in the book is the best bid;

the lowest sell price is the best ask. The difference is the spread, a direct component of trading cost.

- **Depth**: At each price level, there may be multiple resting orders. Depth matters because large market orders may consume several price levels, causing visible price moves.

On top of this, modern markets are *fragmented*:

- The same instrument can trade on multiple exchanges, alternative trading systems, and dark pools.
- Each venue has its own fees, latency, and participant mix.
- Visible liquidity at the best bid and ask on one venue may not represent the full liquidity available across the ecosystem.

An execution agent must therefore solve at least three problems:

- How to choose *when* to trade (timing and scheduling).
- How to choose *how* to trade (order types and sizes).
- How to choose *where* to trade (venue selection and routing).

All of this must be done while abiding by pre-defined safety constraints, risk limits, and regulatory rules.

From Trade List to Execution Problem

At the end of the strategy layer, we typically have a trade list: "Buy 50,000 shares of Stock A; sell 30,000 shares of Stock B; unwind 100 contracts of Futures C;" and so on. The execution agent treats each desired trade as an *execution problem*:

- A target quantity (or notional) to buy or sell.
- A completion horizon (e.g., "by end of day," "within 30 minutes," or "as soon as possible").

- A set of constraints (maximum participation rate, price limits, allowable venues).
- A utility or objective (minimize cost relative to a benchmark price, minimize slippage, control inventory risk, or some combination).

The central task is to decide, for each trade:

> *How do we break this large parent order into a sequence of child orders over time and venues, such that we achieve the target size while managing cost, risk, and information leakage?*

This is where execution algorithms—VWAP, participation-of-volume, arrival-price (implementation shortfall), and custom strategies—come into play.

Execution Agents as a Bridging Layer

Conceptually, an execution agent sits between the portfolio system and the exchange gateways:

- Upstream, it receives trade instructions from the strategy layer, usually in a batch at regular intervals (for example, once per day) or continuously for higher-frequency strategies.
- Downstream, it sends individual orders to venues, listens to acknowledgments and fills, and updates its internal view of remaining inventory.
- In the middle, it maintains an internal model of market conditions and adapts its behavior accordingly.

Immediately after introducing this bridging role, it is useful to visualize the architecture.

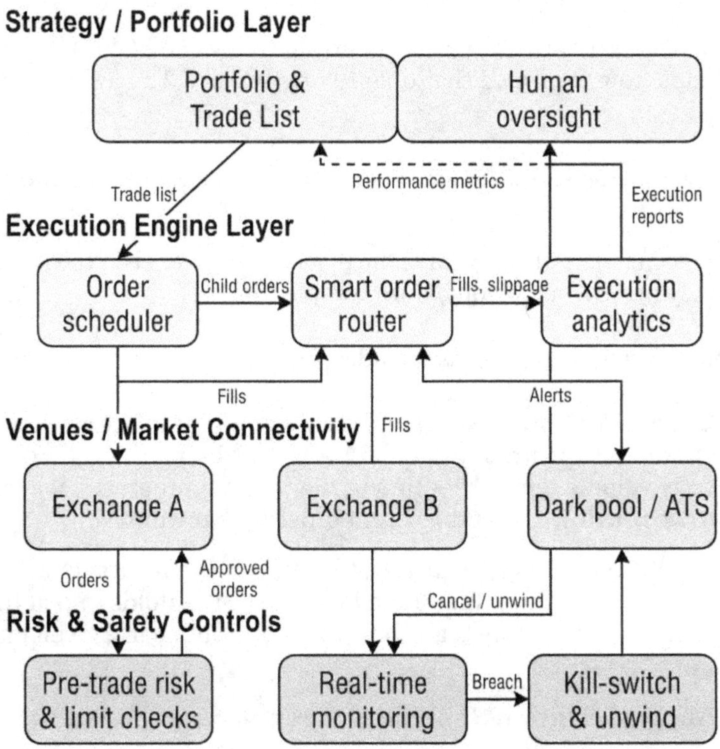

This architecture emphasizes three aspects:

- A clear *interface* between portfolio decisions and execution logic.
- A modular execution engine with scheduling, routing, and analytics components.
- A cross-cutting safety layer that can intercept, monitor, and, if necessary, halt trading.

We now explore these elements in more detail.

Order Scheduling: When and How Fast to Trade

Given a parent order (say, buy 100,000 shares by end of day), the first decision is how to spread that quantity over time. The agent faces a trade-off:

- Trading too *fast* can increase market impact and reveal information.
- Trading too *slowly* exposes the portfolio to price risk; the market may move against you before completion.

Common scheduling patterns include:

- **VWAP (Volume-Weighted Average Price)**: The agent aims to match the intraday volume profile of the market. If 10% of daily volume typically occurs in the first 30 minutes, it will also trade roughly 10% of the parent order in that window.
- **Participation-of-Volume (PoV)**: The agent targets a fixed percentage of the actual traded volume as it unfolds in real time (e.g., "never be more than 10% of market volume in a given interval").
- **Implementation Shortfall**: The agent balances speed versus impact to minimize the difference between the final execution price and a benchmark (often the price at the time the decision was made).

An execution agent often supports several scheduling templates, with parameters chosen by the strategy layer or by a human trader. Generative AI components can help by:

- Analyzing historical execution data to suggest reasonable participation rates for different liquidity regimes.
- Automatically describing the risk-cost trade-off of different schedules in natural language.
- Flagging when the realized volume profile deviates from expectations and suggesting adjustments.

Importantly, the agent should never autonomously select an aggressive schedule outside a predefined, approved menu. AI assistance remains within bounded choices.

Order Types and Smart Order Routing

Once the schedule specifies how much to trade in each time slice, the agent must decide *how* to place that slice into the market and *where* to send it.

Order type selection

Key order types include:

- **Limit orders**: Provide price control but no guarantee of execution; can capture spread if filled passively.
- **Market orders**: Guarantee execution (subject to liquidity) but may cross multiple price levels, paying spreads and impact.
- **Pegged and hidden orders**: Track reference prices or hide size to reduce information leakage, where supported and allowed.

The agent's logic typically prefers passive or slightly aggressive limit orders in liquid markets and resorts to more aggressive orders in illiquid or time-critical situations. Rules might resemble:

- Start passively at or slightly inside the spread.
- If not filled after a timeout, step price closer to the opposite side.
- Avoid posting too visibly if the order represents a large fraction of average daily volume.

Smart order routing across venues

Because liquidity is fragmented, the agent must also decide which venue(s) to use for each child order. A smart order router (SOR) aims to:

- **Consolidate information** from different venues (quotes, depths, fees, and historical fill probabilities).
- **Route** portions of the order to venues offering the best combination of price, likelihood of fill, and cost.
- **Adapt** as conditions change (e.g., if one venue suddenly becomes thin or starts rejecting orders).

At a minimum, the SOR should:

- Respect venue-specific rules (tick sizes, lot sizes, trading halts).
- Enforce venue whitelists/blacklists mandated by compliance.
- Maintain per-venue exposure limits to avoid concentration risk.

Generative AI agents can assist by transforming complex, multi-venue statistics into interpretable summaries (e.g., "Exchange B has recently shown higher adverse selection; consider reducing exposure there") and by proposing updates to routing preferences under human review.

Managing Latency and Market Impact

Execution agents operate at time scales ranging from milliseconds (for quote monitoring and order placement) to minutes or hours (for full order completion). Two intertwined concerns dominate at these scales: *latency* and *market impact*.

Latency considerations

Latency is the delay between observing market data, deciding on an action, and that action affecting the market. For an execution agent:

- Lower latency improves the chance that a limit order priced at the current best bid/ask actually posts at that level before it moves.
- Excessive latency can cause "stale" decisions, where the order is no longer appropriate by the time it arrives.

Design implications include:

- Separating low-latency, deterministic decision paths (e.g., simple price checks, cancels, and modifies) from slower, AI-assisted analytics that run in the background.
- Locating critical components (such as SOR and risk checks) close to exchange gateways to reduce round-trip time, when appropriate.
- Avoiding complex external calls (e.g., to LLM APIs) on the critical path of order placement.

Market impact and information leakage

Market impact occurs when your own trading moves prices, either mechanically (by consuming liquidity) or informationally (others infer that "someone big is buying"). Execution agents manage impact by:

- Limiting participation rate in short intervals.
- Randomizing order sizes and timing within constraints to avoid predictable patterns.
- Breaking large orders into smaller child orders, possibly across venues.
- Being more passive in thin markets and around known liquidity events (e.g., auction opens/closes).

Generative AI-based monitors can help detect unusual patterns—such as adversarial behavior from other participants or sudden increases in impact relative to historical norms—and suggest that the agent slow down or temporarily halt trading.

Embedding Risk and Safety Guardrails

Because execution systems directly touch the market, they must be surrounded by robust risk and safety controls. These are not optional extras; they are core components of the architecture.

Pre-trade checks

Before any order leaves the firm, the agent should apply pre-trade checks such as:

- **Size limits**: Maximum size per order and per instrument; checks based on portfolio, client, and firm-wide caps.
- **Price bands**: Reject or adjust orders with prices too far from current market levels.
- **Credit and margin checks**: Ensure the trade is feasible given available capital and risk limits.
- **Regulatory checks**: Short-sale locate verification, restricted lists, and jurisdiction-specific rules.

These checks are deterministic and auditable. Generative AI may assist in *specifying* and *documenting* them, but not in deciding whether to apply them for any given order.

Real-time monitoring

Once trading is underway, real-time monitoring tracks:

- Execution quality metrics (slippage, fill rates, rejections).
- Exposure metrics (per-asset and aggregate positions, leverage).
- Anomalies (spikes in rejected orders, unusual latency, broken market data feeds).

Here, generative AI can add value by:

- Aggregating and explaining alerts: instead of a flood of low-level warnings, produce a concise narrative ("Latency has doubled on Exchange A; routing has been automatically reduced; here is likely cause X").
- Clustering and classifying incidents across days to spot recurring infrastructure or venue issues.
- Assisting post-mortem analysis by summarizing logs and highlighting key intervals.

Kill-switches and controlled unwinds

Finally, the system must have mechanisms to stop or slow down trading if something goes wrong. Examples include:

- **Global kill-switch**: Immediately cancel all open orders and prevent new ones from being sent.
- **Strategy-level kill-switch**: Disable trading for a specific strategy or client while others continue.
- **Controlled unwind**: Gradually reduce positions to safer levels after an incident, within predefined risk and market impact guidelines.

Triggers might include:

- Breaches of predefined loss or exposure thresholds.
- Severe infrastructure failures (loss of data feeds, connectivity to primary venues).
- Detected inconsistencies between portfolio and execution systems.

Kill-switch logic should be simple, testable, and not subject to on-the-fly modification by AI components. Generative AI can, however, explain why a kill-switch was activated and help coordinate human response.

Testing and Simulation Before Going Live

Because bugs in execution systems can be extremely costly, rigorous testing and simulation are non-negotiable. Good practice includes:

- **Unit and integration tests**: For routing logic, risk checks, and order state management.
- **Replay environments**: Simulating historical days by feeding recorded market data into the execution agent and observing how it would have behaved.
- **Paper trading / shadow mode**: Running the agent live but without sending real orders, comparing its hypothetical actions with actual market outcomes.

Generative AI agents can act as "testing assistants":

- Generating test plans and edge-case scenarios based on system descriptions.
- Inspecting logs from simulated runs and summarizing deviations from expected behavior.
- Helping to maintain human-readable documentation that stays synchronized with evolving code and configuration.

Putting It All Together

Execution agents are the hands and feet of a trading system. They do not decide *what* the portfolio should be—that is the domain of the strategy and portfolio-construction layer—but they largely determine *how much* of the theoretical alpha survives contact with real markets.

For generative-AI-enabled trading stacks, the guiding design principle is consistent with earlier sections:

- Use generative models for *analysis, explanation, and orchestration* around a robust, deterministic execution core.

- Keep safety-critical logic—risk checks, order constraints, kill-switches—simple, transparent, and thoroughly tested.
- Design clean interfaces between layers so that strategy agents, execution agents, and oversight tools can evolve somewhat independently while remaining aligned through configuration and monitoring.

In the next section, we will revisit adaptivity from a different angle: how reinforcement learning and online-learning ideas can be used, carefully and under tight constraints, to adjust both strategy and execution behavior as markets evolve, without compromising risk control.

7.3 Reinforcement Learning and Adaptive Trading

In the first two sections of this chapter, we separated *what* the trading system wants to hold (strategy design and portfolio construction) from *how* it actually trades in the market (execution agents and microstructure). Both layers were deliberately designed to be largely *static*: parameters and rules are chosen by research, validated through backtests and simulations, and then deployed in a relatively fixed form.

Real markets, however, are not static. Relationships between signals and returns shift, liquidity conditions change, and the behavior of other participants evolves. An attractive idea is to let agents *adapt*: to learn from ongoing experience and refine either the strategy or the execution policy in response to new data. Reinforcement learning (RL) and online learning provide systematic frameworks for doing this—but in finance, they must be used with particular care.

This section introduces the main concepts and shows how to apply them in trading systems without losing control of risk or falling prey to overfitting. We frame trading and execution as sequential decision problems, outline the design of safe state and action spaces, discuss reward engineering, and describe practical training setups that rely heavily on offline data and realistic simulators. We then turn to lighter-weight online learning tools—such as bandits and meta-parameter tuning—that can provide adaptivity with lower downside. Throughout, we emphasize a recurring theme of this book: generative AI agents are powerful tools for orchestrating experiments, generating ideas, and summarizing diagnostics, but critical decisions about risk limits and policy deployment remain under human and deterministic control.

Trading as a Sequential Decision Problem

Reinforcement learning is built around the idea of an *agent* interacting with an *environment* over time:

- At each time step, the agent observes a **state** describing the environment.
- It chooses an **action**.
- The environment responds with a new state and a **reward**.
- The agent's goal is to choose actions that maximize some measure of long-run reward.

This is a natural fit for many trading problems:

- In **strategy-level decisions**, the state might summarize prices, risk factors, signals, and current portfolio; the action could be to adjust exposures or rebalance.
- In **execution-level decisions**, the state might include recent order book information, remaining quantity to trade, and elapsed time; the action could be to submit, cancel, or modify orders with particular prices and sizes.

The key difference from static optimization is that each decision influences not only immediate outcomes (today's P&L or execution cost) but also future opportunities and risks (inventory, remaining horizon, information leakage). RL provides tools to reason about these tradeoffs in a principled way.

However, unlike typical RL benchmarks (games, robotics), financial trading involves:

- Strong non-stationarity (the statistical properties of returns and order flow can change).
- Limited and costly data (historical samples are finite, and mistakes in live trading cost real money).
- Tight risk and regulatory constraints.

These realities shape how we design RL-based and adaptive agents.

Designing State Representations

The *state* is the information the agent uses to decide what to do next. Good state design strikes a balance between expressiveness and stability.

Strategy-level state

For strategy-level RL or adaptivity, state might include:

- **Market features**: recent returns, volatility estimates, factor values, macro indicators.
- **Signal summaries**: aggregated alpha forecasts, signal dispersion, and recent signal performance.
- **Portfolio information**: current weights, risk exposures, leverage, cash position.
- **Regime indicators**: proxies for market regimes (e.g., "high volatility," "risk-off") derived from statistical clustering or LLM-based analysis of news.

Rather than feeding in thousands of raw features, we typically construct a compact summary that is easier to model and interpret. Generative AI can help here by exploring feature engineering ideas or by clustering historical periods into interpretable regimes, but the final set of state variables should be stable and documented.

Execution-level state

For execution RL, state needs to capture:

- **Order progress**: remaining quantity, time left to deadline, and realized cost so far.
- **Local microstructure**: best bid/ask, spread, recent depth, and short-horizon price trends.
- **Constraints**: current participation rate, whether venue limits are close to binding, and risk flags.

Here, too, we prefer carefully chosen summaries over raw order book snapshots whenever possible. A smaller, well-designed state space reduces overfitting and allows policies to be more interpretable.

Defining Safe and Interpretable Action Spaces

In RL, the *action space* defines what the agent is allowed to do. In finance, this space must be tightly constrained to preserve risk and compliance.

Strategy-level actions

Instead of allowing an RL agent to set arbitrary positions, we often restrict its actions to:

- **Adjusting parameters** of an existing strategy, such as:
  - the risk-aversion coefficient in the optimizer,
  - the strength of turnover penalties,
  - the relative weights on different alpha components within pre-specified bounds.
- **Choosing among a menu** of pre-approved strategy variants (e.g., "defensive," "balanced," "aggressive") that differ in controlled ways.

In other words, the agent does not directly set trades; it nudges a validated portfolio-construction engine within a safe envelope. This "meta-action" style greatly reduces the risk of unexpected behavior.

Execution-level actions

At the execution layer, actions might include:

- Selecting a schedule type (VWAP vs. participation-of-volume) from a small, approved set.
- Choosing relative aggressiveness (more passive vs. more aggressive limit prices) within configured limits.
- Routing between venues within a whitelisted pool, while respecting per-venue limits.

Again, rather than allowing arbitrary order placements, we let the agent choose among parameterized templates. Deterministic safety checks remain in place downstream; RL only influences behavior within those checks.

Reward Design: Balancing Cost, Risk, and Stability

The *reward* function tells the agent what objectives to optimize. Poorly specified rewards are a common source of fragile or pathological RL policies, especially in finance.

Strategy-level rewards

At the strategy level, natural reward components include:

- **Profit and loss** over a given horizon.
- **Risk penalties**, such as volatility, drawdown, or extreme-loss events.
- **Cost and turnover penalties**, reflecting transaction costs and market impact.

A simple example is to define reward for each decision period as a risk-adjusted P&L measure, minus a scaled turnover term. It is often safer to measure reward over slightly longer horizons (e.g., multi-day or multi-week) to reduce noise, though this increases the difficulty of credit assignment (figuring out which decisions caused which outcomes).

Execution-level rewards

For execution policies, reward design focuses on:

- **Slippage or implementation shortfall**: the difference between realized execution price and a reference price (arrival or decision price).
- **Completion risk**: penalties for failing to complete the order on time.
- **Impact proxies**: additional penalties when participation rates are too high or when trading concentrates in illiquid periods.

A typical per-order reward might be the negative of implementation shortfall, with extra negative terms if the agent fails to complete or violates soft participation targets. Hard risk limits (e.g., maximum participation, price bands) still live outside the reward function as separate constraints.

Training RL Policies: Offline First, Online with Caution

In many RL applications, agents learn directly from live interaction. In trading, this approach is usually unacceptable because:

- Live exploration is expensive and risky.
- Market conditions shift, making naive online learning unstable.

Instead, we rely on a staged approach.

Offline training on historical data

The first step is to train and evaluate policies using historical data:

- For **strategy-level** adaptivity, we can simulate how different parameter choices or small adjustments would have performed historically, treating the environment as a sequence of market states and decisions.

- For **execution-level** policies, we can replay historical limit order books or summarized microstructure around actual past orders, and simulate what would have happened under alternative scheduling and routing decisions.

This is the domain of *offline RL*: learning policies from logged data without further exploration. Offline RL is technically challenging because the data reflect the behavior of previous strategies rather than wide-ranging exploration, but it aligns with the realities of finance: we must squeeze as much learning as possible from the data we already have.

Generative AI agents can play a valuable support role:

- Transcribing and organizing historical trading logs into clean training datasets.
- Proposing candidate state representations and reward definitions, and helping researchers interpret ablation studies.
- Summarizing policy behavior under backtest, highlighting regimes and scenarios where performance is strong or weak.

Simulators and synthetic environments

For execution RL in particular, realistic simulators are crucial. A simulator can:

- Emulate order book dynamics, including other participants' behavior.
- Provide a safe environment for agents to explore different order placement and routing strategies.
- Allow controlled stress tests (e.g., sudden liquidity droughts, volatility spikes).

Generative models can assist in building such simulators by:

- Learning statistical models of order flow and price response from historical data.

- Generating realistic but varied scenarios (e.g., different volatility or correlation regimes) that go beyond the limited historical record.

However, we must always remember that simulators are approximations. Policies that look strong in simulation must be further constrained and tested before being trusted with real capital.

Constrained online updates

Only after thorough offline testing and simulation should we consider online adaptation. Even then, we proceed cautiously:

- **Shadow mode**: Run the adaptive policy in parallel with the existing production policy, but do not let it control real trades. Compare their decisions and performance.
- **Gradual ramp-up**: Start by allowing the adaptive policy to control a small fraction of volume or a subset of instruments, increasing only if performance and risk remain acceptable.
- **Strict monitoring and rollback**: Define clear metrics and thresholds that trigger an automatic reversion to the prior, stable policy.

Generative AI tools can help analyze discrepancies between shadow and production policies, explain why the adaptive policy recommends certain changes, and monitor for drift or emerging failure modes.

Online Learning Beyond Full RL

Full reinforcement learning is not the only way to introduce adaptivity. In many trading contexts, simpler online learning methods are more practical and safer.

Bandits for strategy and execution choices

Multi-armed bandit algorithms address problems where we repeatedly choose among a set of options and observe noisy rewards. Examples include:

- Choosing among a few strategy variants (e.g., different alpha weightings or risk-aversion levels).
- Selecting among multiple execution templates (VWAP vs. more aggressive schedules) for similar orders.

Bandit algorithms gradually allocate more weight to better-performing options while still exploring less-used ones. They are simpler than full RL because they do not try to model the long-term effect of state transitions, just average performance of choices.

Meta-parameter tuning

Another practical pattern is to treat the core strategy and execution logic as fixed, but let an adaptive process adjust a handful of hyperparameters over time. For example:

- Gradually adjusting turnover penalties based on recent realized costs.
- Tuning the balance between aggressive and passive execution as liquidity conditions change.
- Adapting the strength of different signals based on their recent out-of-sample performance.

This can be framed as a small-scale RL or bandit problem in itself, but with tight bounds and strong priors based on research. Generative AI agents can help generate candidate parameter schedules, run controlled experiments, and summarize their outcomes in human-friendly language.

Regime detection and switching

Markets often exhibit regimes (e.g., high vs. low volatility, risk-on vs. risk-off). Rather than continuously tweaking parameters, a more structured approach is:

- Use statistical or machine-learning methods to classify the current regime based on state variables and possibly textual signals.
- Maintain a set of pre-validated policies or parameter sets, one for each regime.

- Switch between these policies when credible evidence suggests a regime change.

Here, an LLM-based agent can be particularly useful in integrating qualitative information (news, macro commentary) with quantitative indicators to support regime labeling, while the actual switching logic follows deterministic rules and thresholds agreed upon in advance.

Risk Management and Overfitting in Adaptive Systems

Adaptivity is a double-edged sword. While it promises responsiveness to changing conditions, it also increases the risk of overfitting to noise and amplifying short-term patterns that do not persist.

To mitigate these risks, an adaptive trading stack should:

- **Separate research from deployment**: New adaptive policies must pass through the same research, validation, and approval pipeline as static strategies.
- **Limit degrees of freedom**: Keep state, action, and reward spaces compact and interpretable; avoid high-dimensional black-box policies that are hard to reason about.
- **Enforce hard risk limits**: Position, leverage, margin, and loss limits remain outside the control of adaptive mechanisms and are enforced centrally.
- **Use robust evaluation**: Rely on multiple backtest periods, cross-validation, and stress scenarios, not a single historical window.
- **Continuously monitor**: Track out-of-sample performance relative to baselines, and be willing to dial back adaptivity if it fails to add value.

Generative AI agents can support this by acting as "evaluation assistants," automatically compiling performance reports, spotting patterns in failure cases, and keeping documentation synchronized with the evolving behavior of adaptive components.

The Role of Generative AI in RL-Driven Trading Agents

Across the design choices above, a consistent pattern emerges regarding generative AI:

- **Orchestration**: LLM-based agents help design experiments, configure simulations, schedule backtests, and manage the metadata around policies, datasets, and evaluation metrics.
- **Insight and explanation**: They translate complex RL and online-learning diagnostics—learning curves, value-function estimates, policy heatmaps—into clear narratives for risk committees and portfolio managers.
- **Exploration of ideas**: They propose alternative state representations, reward structures, and action restrictions that researchers can test within the safe, offline environment.

What they do *not* do is autonomously override risk controls, expand action spaces without approval, or deploy new policies directly into production. Those steps require explicit human sign-off and must pass through robust, deterministic pipelines.

By treating reinforcement learning and online learning as carefully bounded layers around a stable core of portfolio construction and execution logic, we can allow trading agents to adapt to evolving markets while keeping risk and overfitting under control. This balance—between learning and discipline, between automation and oversight—is central to building trustworthy generative-AI-enabled trading systems.

www.ingramcontent.com/pod-product-compliance
Lightning Source LLC
LaVergne TN
LVHW020314061026
849616LV00032B/408